Haunted Places
of Bedfordshire and Buckinghamshire

Rupert Matthews

COUNTRYSIDE BOOKS
NEWBURY, BERKSHIRE

First Published 2004
© Rupert Matthews, 2004

COUNTRYSIDE BOOKS
3 Catherine Road
Newbury, Berkshire

To view our complete range of books,
please visit us at
www..countrysidebooks.co.uk

ISBN 1 85306 886 1

Cover painting supplied by
Anthony Wallis

Designed by Peter Davies, Nautilus Design
Typeset by Mac Style Ltd, Scarborough, N. Yorkshire
Produced through MRM Associates Ltd., Reading
Printed by J W Arrowsmith Ltd., Bristol

·Contents·

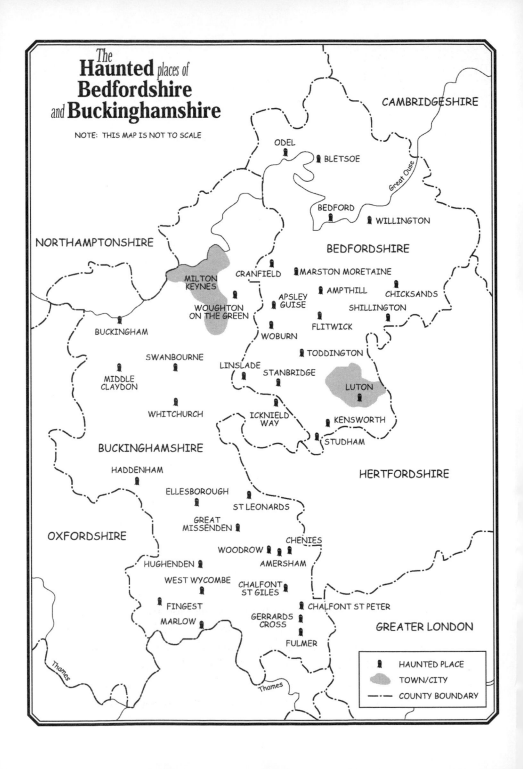

• Introduction •

That ghosts exist, there can be little doubt. What they actually are is another matter completely. During my researches for this book I think that I came across almost as many ideas about what a ghost is as I did reports of ghosts.

One witness who gave me a remarkably clear account of her meeting with the Grey Lady of Luton ended by saying, 'Well, there you are. I suppose I just imagined the whole thing.'

Another person who caught but the most fleeting of glimpses of the ghostly horseman of Gerrards Cross was keen to talk at length about the meaning of the sighting in philosophical terms which were, I must admit, a bit beyond me.

No matter. There are ghosts abroad in Bedfordshire and Buckinghamshire, and there are hundreds of people who will bear witness to the fact.

And it must be said that finding ghosts in these two counties was remarkably easy. All areas of Britain have their spooks and spectres, but few have such a diverse range as do Bedfordshire and Buckinghamshire. Of course, I had a bit of a head start with a mother-in-law who lives in Bedfordshire. I always knew that I had married into a gregarious family, but it was not until I started asking about local ghosts that I realised quite how wide their social contacts spread.

I was directed to a lady from the sewing circle at Flitwick, a fellow enthusiast for vegetable gardening from Bletsoe and many more. And, of course, 'everyone knows about Chicksands'. I thank my in-laws for their help and patience in the research of this book. I would also thank my daughter, whose squeals from the back seat of the car and occasional demands for food, drink or a clean nappy provided endless distractions from the task in hand.

But the good folk of the counties must be thanked as well. No one looked at me askance in the course of my wanderings. Most were happy to talk about their local phantoms or their own encounters with the supernatural. They showed me the sites of the hauntings and even drew sketches of what they had seen.

But the true stars of this book are the counties themselves. Bedfordshire and Buckinghamshire are lovely places to visit and to drive around in search of ghosts and phantoms. Those who think that these counties are too close to London to be of much interest do them a disservice. There are many rural corners tucked away here and there that the passing centuries have barely touched.

I hope you enjoy reading about the haunted places of Bedfordshire and Buckinghamshire, but I recommend that you take every opportunity to go and see them too. Then you will come to enjoy the beauties of these counties for yourself.

Rupert Matthews

ODELL

The church of All Saints lies just outside the Bedfordshire village of Odell where a steep slope rises up from the road. It is an easy building to find, standing so prominently above the little valley in which Odell lies. Some centuries ago, however, it was not the finding of the church that was causing Sir Roland Alstons trouble, it was getting there.

Sir Roland was the local squire who owned most of the fertile acres around the village, renting out the farms to tenants and living very well on the proceeds. But he was not a particularly nice man. Indeed, with his drunken rages, wild

Sir Roland Alstons of Odell was a quarrelsome man, always ready to pick a fight.

gambling and taste for loose women he might have been the archetypal wicked squire of English folklore. Where he differed, though, from so many others of his type was that he had the most extraordinary luck. Despite his gambling, he never lost his estates and although his temper got him into numerous fights he never suffered serious harm. It was, locals whispered behind his back, as if he had the luck of the Devil.

And on one terrible day, it turned out that that was exactly what he had.

It was, as might be guessed, a dark and stormy night when a stranger came calling at the home of Sir Roland. The new arrival was tall, dressed in the most magnificently tailored outfit and mounted on a great black stallion. He knocked peremptorily on the door and demanded admittance from the maid who answered. Sweeping in as if he knew the house well, though the girl had never before seen him, the stranger strode into Sir Roland's private rooms.

Somewhat nervously, the butler entered to see if any food or drink should be prepared to make the stranger welcome. He found Sir Roland sitting bolt upright in his chair staring at the visitor with evident terror. The stranger, however, was all suave politeness as he turned down the butler's offer on the grounds that he would not be staying long. The butler withdrew.

A few silent, tense minutes passed while the servants gathered in the hall. Then the doors flew open and out burst Sir Roland. He ran past his servants, dashed out through the front doorway and sprang onto the stranger's black stallion. The visitor sauntered out in his wake, laughing. 'You can't outrun me,' the man shouted. Then he set off in pursuit, sprinting faster than the servants had ever seen mortal man run.

A few minutes later, a villager saw Sir Roland galloping at high speed down the lane towards the church, pursued by the stranger. Then the pair were gone.

Next morning, when Sir Roland had not returned home, the servants set out to search for him. Hearing that he had been riding for the church, they made their way there. The door was locked and bolted from the inside, while the outside was marked by five burn marks that had not been there the day before. A window was prised open and a boy pushed in through the narrow gap. He found Sir Roland dead just inside the door with a look of abject terror on his face.

It was never entirely certain what had happened, but one theory quickly took hold and became accepted as truth. Sir Roland, it was believed, had sold his soul to the Devil. This would explain his wild ways and incredible luck over the years. And the mysterious stranger can have been none other than the Evil One himself, come to collect the debt. Sir Roland must have realised his only chance was to get on to holy ground. Had he made it in time? Nobody knew. They gave him a decent Christian burial, just in case.

All Saints' church, Odell, the scene of a terrifying encounter
that has been recreated regularly in spectral form.

The story of Sir Roland was the talk of the county for months, but then it faded from people's thoughts as these things do. Much later, ten years to the day since that fatal night, the ghost of Sir Roland returned. Mounted on the black stallion, he tore again through the night. Galloping as if hell itself were at his heels, the phantom squire raced through the village, rode up to the church doors and ran into the building. And then the Devil really did appear. No smartly dressed stranger this, but the apparition of a demon with horns, tail and cloven hooves. Laughing loudly, the terrifying creature sauntered to the church doors, paused and then vanished.

This blood-chilling phantom drama was played out regularly every ten years for more than a century. Then the hauntings became rather less regular. Sometimes the ghosts returned twice in a year, then decades would pass before they were seen again. They do not seem to have disturbed the peace of Odell for well over 20 years now. Perhaps Sir Roland has found rest at last.

Or perhaps he will be back some day to terrify the good folk of Odell and once again bring hell to earth in his wake.

BLETSOE

The village of Bletsoe lies off the A6, rather than on it, and may be easily missed by travellers. This was just as well back in 1745 when a foreign army came to England for the last time, namely the force of Scottish Highlanders raised by Bonnie Prince Charlie, which had defeated the British army in Scotland and was now marching down what is now the A6 towards London. While troops were rushed back from the wars in Europe, panic ran ahead of the Highlanders who reached Derby. Even as far south as Bletsoe, villagers hurried to bury valuables to keep them out of the way of pillaging Scots and sent their womenfolk away to safety.

Standing directly on the main road north, and so in the path of the enemy, was the Falcon Inn. This was one of the most famous and best admired

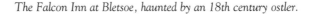

The Falcon Inn at Bletsoe, haunted by an 18th century ostler.

coaching inns on the road to Leicester, Derby and Scotland. The Scots never reached this far, but the Falcon played host to the military officers racing back and forth between London and the troops facing the Scots. When the army marched north, the troops camped around the inn and the innkeeper did booming business.

It may have been in these troubled times that the ostler who worked here came to have an unfortunate accident. At least, it was recorded as an accident though local gossip had it otherwise. The poor lad was found dead, having apparently fallen from the hayloft. Whatever the truth of his death, the boy returns to the inn to this day. He is sometimes seen in the gardens, which run down to the river, but most often appears in the pub itself. For some reason he seems to favour the rooms that are now the kitchens, where food is freshly prepared lunchtimes and evenings for the customers.

The ghost is blamed for things that go missing, which may or may not be his fault, and is generally reckoned to be one of the more active phantoms in Bedfordshire.

BEDFORD

As the county town, Bedford has a history going back well over a thousand years. It is home to several fine public buildings, bridges and town houses. It has also long been the centre for royal justice in the region and it is this that led to the most persistent haunting in the town.

Black Tom was, everyone agreed, a rogue. He was a likeable enough young man who caused little actual harm to anyone – but he did lighten their pockets of silver and gold on occasion. It therefore came as no surprise to anyone when Black Tom was one day arrested and thrown into Bedford Prison. Nor was it much of a shock that he was sentenced to death, this being the official sentence for highway robbery and a host of other crimes in the later 18th century. It was a bit of a surprise, however, that he was actually hanged.

At the time it was usual for the judges and magistrates to retire after a trial to await any pleas for mercy from the condemned person, their relatives or any

All Bedford knew Black Tom to be a rogue, but there was much surprise when a court sent him to the gallows.

interested local residents. Depending on the severity of the crime, and the eloquence of the pleas or size of the petition, the sentence was adjusted. Most people sentenced to death were not hanged. Instead they were imprisoned for a set number of years, sent to work as convict labour in the colonies or fined. Being a non-violent robber and, moreover, a ready wit, Black Tom had no trouble getting a good petition together signed by the people of Bedford. But he was hanged anyway.

On his way to the gallows on a cart, Black Tom was stopped by the landlord of the inn that stood by the town gates on the main road north. On being offered a bottle of wine, Black Tom drank a glass, then handed the rest of the bottle to his friends. 'I'll pay for it on my way back,' he joked to the landlord. It was the last joke the witty rogue ever made.

It turned out that the head gaoler of Bedford Prison had not passed on the petition to the judges so they had not, therefore, commuted the sentence. He had obviously not been given a suitably large bribe by the impoverished Black Tom. This, and other scandals, appalled a Bedford gentleman by the name of John Howard. He discovered that most county authorities did not pay their gaolers a salary, but instead expected them to earn money by charging prisoners for food and drink and by taking bribes. This, Howard decided, could lead only to injustices, corruption and degradation.

Having travelled around England to collect evidence, Howard began to lobby Parliament for reform. It was a slow process, but in 1774 he succeeded in having an Act of Parliament passed that for the first time set down basic levels of sanitation, food and care in prisons and made provision for gaolers to be paid a salary to supply them.

It was all too late for poor Black Tom, but although he is gone he is not forgotten. Nor has he forgotten Bedford. He still returns from time to time in spectral form to the spot where he was hanged. The place is now a roundabout where Union Street joins the A6 a little north of the town centre. Tom stands quietly beside the road, often with head bowed, and is sometimes mistaken for some local in fancy dress.

Another haunting with judicial links takes place in the imposing Magistrates Court on St Paul's Square. It is generally thought that the ghost haunting this building is the same phantom who plagues the Clerk's Offices in Mill Street. This is a former Clerk to the Court who died suddenly when on duty after many long years of dutiful service. He is rarely seen, but makes his presence felt by slamming doors, stomping up the stairs and generally giving rise to supernatural noises around the place.

The roundabout in Bedford that marks the site of the old gallows,
to which Black Tom returns from time to time.

More visible, but just as enigmatic, is the gentleman in tweeds who is seen near the Methodist Chapel in Newnham Avenue. He stands there quite clearly, dressed in a tweed jacket and dark trousers of distinctly 1920s cut, but who he might be is completely unknown. Nobody who has seen him recognises him and no stories are attached to him. The gentleman in tweeds just walks by the chapel, then is gone.

* * *

A short distance outside Bedford is the little village of Ravensden. It is not the village here that is haunted, but the lane running north. The phantom likely to be encountered on this lane is rather disturbing, and some say distinctly evil. She is an elderly woman dressed in a long black dress, perhaps more of a cloak. Many who see her think she is a harmless old soul. It is only when she looks at somebody that the evil manifests itself. The woman's face is contorted into such an expression of hatred that it startles those who see it.

Why the woman should be so angry is not entirely clear. Some say she is a witch who was turned out of her home for various unspecified crimes in the 17th century and who died of exposure at the roadside. Others maintain she is just some wicked old woman and explain no further. All agree that it best to avoid her for her mere look brings bad luck.

Nearby again is the village of Wilden, which may be haunted by the same ghost as the road out of Ravensden. The two sound remarkably similar, both being wicked old ladies dressed in black. In Wilden, the ghost walks from the church to the old manor rather than frequenting isolated lanes, but is otherwise identical.

Perhaps there are two phantom women in black lurking in the same small area of Bedfordshire, but it seems unlikely.

WILLINGTON

In past centuries the favour of the monarch could bring all sorts of lucrative rewards, some more respectable than others. Few knew this better than did Sir John Gostwick of Willington in the 16th century.

The Gostwick, sometimes spelled Gostwicke, family had lived around Willington for generations before Sir John was born. The parish church contains tombs of the family that chart their varying fortunes through the opulence or simplicity of their decoration. Sir John, however, not content with the steady if unremarkable income to be had as a landowner amongst the minor gentry, took himself off to London and used what contacts he had to get himself accepted at the court of Henry VIII. He at once set about making himself both popular and useful. If any royal official had a tedious task to perform, Sir John was happy to undertake it. If a dull meeting clashed with an enjoyable social event, Sir John was willing to go to the meeting in the place of whoever should really have been there. All such duties were carried out efficiently and with a ready smile. No task was too demanding nor too boring for him.

The magnificent dovecote at Willington.

Soon royal officials came to rely on Sir John. It was so easy to ask him to do the work rather than do it for themselves. So when Sir John mentioned that he really ought to return to his lands around Willington to attend to business, it came as quite a shock. Those same officials began to find some paid, but not terribly onerous, tasks for Sir John that would keep him at court. So when a more permanent post came along, it was natural to give it to Sir John. He was, after all, helpful and obliging. By such means did Sir John get himself appointed to the post of Master of the Hounds to the King.

Looking after the royal hunting dogs was not the most glamorous nor the best paid appointment at court. But Henry was a passionate huntsman and he took a great interest in his hounds. Which meant that he spent a lot of time talking to Sir John about which dogs were fit, and which were ill, where to find the best game and so forth. Before long, it was widely known that Sir John Gostwick had the King's ear. Anyone who wanted a matter brought to the King's attention would seek out Sir John, who was, as ever, most helpful and supportive. He happily mentioned things to the King in passing, or brought up subjects in conversation. Of course, Sir John asked for a small fee in return and everyone was willing to pay the trifles he requested.

Sir John was never greedy. He never asked too much in payment, nor did he push a subject too hard upon the monarch. In this way he kept his position at court when others lost theirs, and sometimes their heads as well. And all the while he was slowly building up his fortune. He spent it on his property in Willington. The old manor was torn down and replaced with a magnificent mansion in the very latest style. The house, sadly, burned down in the 18th century, but the stables and dovecote remain. The sheer scale and grandeur of these domestic buildings give some indication of the splendour of Sir John's home.

The ghostly squire of Willington walks across this field towards the church.

It is no surprise to learn that Sir John returns to Willington in spectral form. He walks slowly around the site of his old home, now replaced by a Georgian house, and strolls to view his dovecote and stables. He has even been seen making his way to the church, which houses his family tombs.

Two generations after Sir John's death the Gostwicks married into the family of the Dukes of Bedford and the estates passed to that family. Willington was rebuilt to be a model agricultural village, and the regular layout and neat houses remain to this day. As does Sir John's phantom.

CRANFIELD

The village of Cranfield is best known for its links to the Royal Air Force. During World War II this was a large air base from which flew nightfighters protecting Britain from the Luftwaffe. Cranfield was later converted into a training base for men of the RAF Bomber Command who were to bomb the enemy beyond the English Channel. All too many of these men did not return to Cranfield, and some of those who did died of their wounds and now rest in Cranfield churchyard. After the war Cranfield Airfield was dedicated to the study of aeronautics and is now a university research facility.

The ghost that haunts the village, however, has nothing to do with the gallant airmen of Cranfield, but is much older. Some three centuries ago the manor of Cranfield was in the hands of Lord Snaggs. This Lord Snaggs was not, it would seem, a bad fellow. But he was acquisitive and quickly snapped up the chance to marry the orphaned heiress of a neighbouring family. He thus managed to acquire considerable estates, but also a young wife for whom he did not care overmuch.

The new Lady Snaggs had hoped for stability and affection from her older husband, but instead found he was more interested in her acres than in her. After a few years had passed by, Lady Snaggs developed an interest in one of the more handsome of the young farmhands who worked the spreading acres of her husband's lands. For a while the clandestine romance blossomed. But then on a bright, moonlit night, things took a tragic turn for the worse. The farmhand was waiting for Lady Snaggs at a regular meeting point along Wood End Road. Although the young man waited until well past midnight, Lady Snaggs never arrived. Assuming she had been delayed for some reason, the lad cut across the fields to his home.

Next morning, Lord Snaggs announced that his wife was missing and sent his servants out far and wide to raise a search party to find her. It did not take long. The bloodied, decapitated body of the beautiful Lady Snaggs lay in the middle of Wood End Road. Her jewellery had been stripped from her lifeless body. It appeared to be the work of a gang of robbers, who had turned violent when Lady Snaggs had resisted their demands for her jewels.

But soon suspicions began to emerge that the death of Lady Snaggs had not been so straightforward. It had been a warm, moonlit summer's night and several villagers had been up late that evening for various reasons. None had seen nor heard a gang of robbers. One had spotted Lady Snaggs' lover walking home across the fields from Wood End Road and reported that fact to the local magistrate. The young man was arrested and his home searched, but neither bloodstained clothes nor jewels were found. Lacking a history of violence, the man was let go. But the secret of the affair had come out. Suspicion now fell on the wronged husband. Lord Snaggs, likewise, had no evidence showing against him and he too was released.

The mystery of what happened in Wood End Road that fatal night

Wood End Road, just outside Cranfield, where the murdered Lady Snaggs still paces restlessly.

remains. Only one person could reveal the facts, and that was Lady Snaggs. She returns in spectral form time and again to the narrow lane where she met her death. Sometimes she is seen headless, other times complete. Always she is pacing restlessly along the stretch of road where her body was found.

Is she searching for the lost jewels, or does she wish to impart the name of her killer? Nobody knows, for none who have seen her have yet had the courage to ask.

MARSTON MORETAINE

The church at Marston Moretaine is unlike any other in Bedfordshire. The tower stands quite separate from the body of the church with a broad swathe of grass lying between the two.

From time to time a dark figure is seen lurking near the tower, which may, in part, explain the stories that have grown up around this curious construction. According to one account, the tower was originally built in conventional fashion, attached to the church. But then one day, many years ago, the Devil came to Marston Moretaine to take his revenge on the overly prayerful folk of the village. He grabbed the tower, of which the good Christian folk were so proud, and hefted it up on his back. At this point the vicar appeared, saw what the Devil was up to and fell to his knees in prayer. The tower instantly grew so heavy that the Devil was forced to drop it. He had carried the structure only a short distance, and so it remains where he let it fall.

So furious was the Devil that he was, quite literally, hopping mad with anger. He hopped first into the centre of the village, then hopped again to land beyond the village at a spot to this day known as Leapfield. His third hop took him to an ancient stone circle some distance away where three boys were playing leapfrog. This being the Sabbath, with frivolous games forbidden, the Devil claimed the boys as his own and carried them off to Hell.

Such legends are fanciful. The tower of Marston Moretaine was set separate from the church deliberately by its human builders. No doubt the tales of the

A strange figure lurks in the gap between church and tower at Marston Moretaine.

visit by the Devil were invented to explain the odd position, but that does not explain the shadowy figure seen hereabouts on occasion. If it is not the Devil, then who is it?

•South Bedfordshire•

ASPLEY GUISE

Weathercock Lane in Aspley Guise has changed dramatically since the mid-18th century. Then it was a remote country lane heavily overshadowed by pinewoods and towering holly hedges. It was a dark, foreboding place where any grisly crime seemed likely.

Today, that same lane is broad and busy with through traffic. The road is lined by 20th century houses with open, sunny gardens that are bright with flowers. Yet late at night something of the old grim atmosphere returns, and returns in spectral form.

Weathercock Lane.

The Old Manor still stands, though its surrounding farmlands have long since been sold off for housing developments. The house was built in 1575 using stout timber framing from the local woods and is decorated with some fine wooden panelling and carving. And it was here, in around 1730, that the owner of the manor murdered the local ne'er-do-well who had been presumptuous enough to court his daughter. The killing had been done in a fit

21

of anger when the outraged father found the miscreant and his daughter in bed, and she had also died in the furious attack that followed. In desperation to hide his crime, the man hid the bodies in a secure cupboard in the cellar until he could invent a plausible reason to get the servants out of the house long enough for him to dispose of the bodies properly.

It was, therefore, a great misfortune that the very next night the house should receive an unwelcome visit from a gang of ruffians led by none other than Dick Turpin. Although best known as a highwayman, Turpin would also indulge in burglary, blackmail and fraud if it suited him, and this particular night it was burglary that suited him very well.

With the house owner and servants safely tied up, Turpin and his gang set about searching the property for valuables. The locked cupboard in the cellar proved too tempting a prospect, so Turpin broke it open hoping to find silver or cash. What he found was the dead bodies.

Realising a good, if unscrupulous, opportunity when he saw it, Turpin hurriedly bundled the bodies back into hiding and kept quiet. A few days later, however, he slipped back to Aspley Guise and confronted the murderer with his deeds. Blackmail was the object, and Turpin was most successful. He not only succeeded in extorting cash from the killer, but also a hiding place whenever he chose to call.

More than once Turpin hurried here after holding up a coach on the Leicester road, knowing he would be assured of safe lodgings until the forces of law and order moved on.

Of course, it could not last forever. One of servants became suspicious of the mysterious horseman who would arrive unannounced, stay for a few days helping himself to the finest wines and foods in the house, then ride off just as abruptly. The authorities were informed and, next time he called, Turpin had a difficult escape. In parting, he left behind an account of the murders, which sent the killer to the gallows.

Such is the tale of Weathercock Lane in Aspley Guise. To this day a dark, phantom horseman rides down the lane towards the Old Manor. He is seen late at night, when the road is less busy with traffic than it is usually. Dressed in a tricorn hat and a long, dark coat, the rider trots unhurriedly down the lane. It is generally supposed that the ghostly horseman is Turpin himself, but the identification is not certain. It may be that the dramatic events at the Old Manor have caused Turpin's name to be attached to the ghost of a quite different man. After all, there are no obvious features of a highwayman about the rider – he carries no pistols nor wears a mask.

Whoever the phantom rider may be, he is probably none too impressed to be linked to murder, blackmail and burglary. Unless, of course, he really is Dick Turpin in which case he would not care too much. Turpin was like that.

WOBURN ABBEY

Woburn Abbey is without doubt one of the premier stately homes of England. The grounds are magnificent, the house splendid and the artworks within fabulous.

As its name suggests, Woburn began life as a Cistercian monastery. The religious house was confiscated by Henry VIII in 1538 during the Reformation that so disrupted religious life in England. Having stripped the place of its movable wealth, Henry granted the lands and buildings to his Lord Privy Seal. Lord John Russell, later to be made Earl of Bedford by King Edward VI, took down many of the monastic buildings and remodelled the remainder to be a comfortable home. In 1744 the Russells, now holding the title of Duke of Bedford, tore down the old house and commissioned first John Sanderson and then Henry Flitcroft to create an entirely new residence. It is this graceful Georgian house that is the Woburn Abbey of today.

The oldest ghost of Woburn dates back to the traumatic upheavals of the Reformation. Most monks, nuns and abbots who lost their holy houses during the Dissolution of the Monasteries were not treated badly. They were moved to almshouses or given modest pensions so that they would not starve, but were forbidden to continue their religious life. The last Abbot of Woburn did not take his fate so meekly. Not only did he rail against the soldiers sent to seize the Abbey and its assets, he denounced King Henry as a heretic and worse. The tough soldiers hanged him from an oak tree beside the church without much ado. The figure of this cleric was seen for many years standing beneath the tree, which was surrounded by a patch of barren ground where no grass would grow. This particular ghost has not been reported since the tree died and was felled some generations ago.

The next oldest of the Woburn phantoms lurks in the private chambers of the house, where it manifests itself by stalking through the lounge, not that it is ever seen. First the door on one side of the room flies open and slams shut, then the sound of footsteps moves across the room to a second door,

The entrance to Woburn Abbey, one of the finest, and most haunted, stately homes of England.

which opens and shuts. During the 1960s this ghostly activity became so frequent that the ducal family moved their television to another room where they stood more chance of watching a programme uninterrupted.

This ghost is traditionally said to be that of a black servant of the 3rd Duke of Bedford who met a grisly end in the room just after the present house had been built. Reasoning that the house must contain a wealth of precious objects, a gang of thieves broke in and began quietly searching cupboards for silver and other valuables. They had reached this lounge when the black servant came across them. The bandits quickly overpowered the man and bound him to a chair. Rather than waste more time searching, the crooks decided to beat the servant to make him reveal the locations of the most valuable objects. Loyally, he refused to answer, despite the violence, so they threw him out of the window to his death.

Such an unpleasant death would explain why anyone might return as a phantom, but it is not entirely clear why he should want to stomp about slamming doors.

Considerably more gentle is the spectre to be found flitting around the grounds, especially near the summerhouse. This is the phantom of Lady Mary Tribe, who married the 11th Duke and so came to live at Woburn. Lady Mary was an adventurous woman who in the 1920s became involved in the glamorous business of flying. She was the first woman to fly to South Africa, visiting many remote British colonial settlements on the way, and she made great efforts to encourage other women to take to the air for both sport and employment. Unfortunately the Flying Duchess, as she was known, lost her life in 1937 when flying off the coast of East Anglia. Soon afterwards her ghostly counterpart was seen drifting gently around Woburn grounds. She is seen

An early military flying machine. It was on aircraft such as this that the 'Flying Duchess' learned to fly in the 1920s.

dressed in a pretty summer frock as if ready to entertain her aristocratic friends at a garden party. The flying togs are nowhere to be seen.

The Flying Duchess is not the only duchess to haunt Woburn. The 6th Duchess held court here in the early 19th century as a noted hostess. She has been seen infrequently in one of the reception rooms. The most recent sighting came in 2004, when she was mistaken by a visitor to the house for a guide.

Perhaps as intriguing is the ghost of the Butler's Pantry. This figure is ill defined and appears blurred, but is usually said to have the appearance of a monk. Given the indistinct nature of the ghost, it is not entirely certain that it is a shade of one of the holy men who used to live at Woburn. Because of the location, this seems more likely to be a phantom servant of the Bedfords. He is, in any case, not seen often.

Woburn Abbey has been one of the finest stately homes of England for generations and, in more recent years, a top ranking tourist attraction. It would seem to be a favourite haunt for the ghosts of Bedfordshire as well.

AMPTHILL

The mighty fortress of Ampthill Castle is no more, but a ghost still haunts the stronghold. He is one of the more dramatic apparitions of Bedfordshire, but does not always appear in his full glory.

People in Ampthill who know about the ghost of Great Park will cheerfully confirm that he is a most splendid fellow. A knight dressed in a suit of shining armour, carrying a shield boldly painted with a colourful coat of arms and carrying a lance from which streams

The phantom knight of Ampthill is said to ride in full armour and with pennon streaming.

a brightly decorated pennant, he gallops out of the old ruins, down a long disused road and disappears close to a stream.

This sounds a truly spectacular phantom to rank alongside England's best. However, those who have actually seen the ghostly knight of Ampthill are not too sure. They report a more insubstantial phantom. It is, without doubt, a ghostly horseman but he seems to be a misty, grey shape rather than a definite knight in armour.

Perhaps he was once as magnificent as local talk has it, but he has faded with the years. Some ghosts do that.

FLITWICK

The Swan public house is best described as being a traditional pub. The ghost, however, is more indefinable than most. Flitwick, itself, is one of those villages that until the mid-20th century had not changed much in hundreds of years. Thatched cottages crowded round a green, a medieval church had benefited from Victorian restoration and the 17th century manor house was home to the local gentry. Even the River Flitt was largely untouched, flowing through unstrengthened banks and forming wide flood meadows where rare bog plants grew in profusion.

The cottages, green, church, manor and rare plants remain, but Flitwick has changed radically. Large new housing estates have sprung up

The Swan at Flitwick has been the focus for some genial ghostly activity.

to cater for the rapidly increasing population. Many of these folk work in London, or in nearby satellite towns, but a good few of them go to the Swan to drink and eat.

And most welcoming the Swan is too. So is its ghost. The phantom is said to play host to a number of tricks. He will hide things, move objects around and suchlike pranks. Generally it is newcomers who attract his attention. Any new member of staff can expect their jackets or belongings to be moved unexpectedly. Disconcerting, some might think, but that is how the ghost is said to go about things.

CHICKSANDS PRIORY

That Chicksands Priory is haunted nobody in the area has any doubt. That the ghost is female everybody, again, agrees. But beyond that there is disagreement over details and origins.

According to the most often told version of the story, the ghost is that of a nun. Back in 1534, Henry VIII was looking for excuses to close down the monasteries so that he could take control of their lands and wealth for his own purposes. The man tasked with finding reasons for the move was Thomas Cromwell, who had risen from being the son of a brewer to become Chancellor of the Exchequer through his hard work and skill with figures. Cromwell knew his task would be easier if he could gather evidence, or even mere gossip, that the monks and nuns were not as holy as they should be.

Cromwell was, therefore, delighted to hear from a member of the local gentry, Richard Layton, that the monks of Chicksands Priory had a dark secret to hide. It seems that they acted as teachers and trainers to novices from other nearby religious houses and were supposed to instil in these youngsters the love of Christ and knowledge of the scriptures. But one monk had instilled a quite different sort of love in a novice nun, and the knowledge he taught her did not bear repeating – or so said Mr Layton.

In time, the novice fell pregnant and the Prior of Chicksands was presented with a problem. The errant monk was sent off on a pilgrimage that would keep him safely out of the country for months, but the young girl was another matter. She had not yet taken her vows and so could not be packed off abroad without her parents' consent – and given the circumstances they were hardly likely to agree. Nor could the girl be relied upon to have her child, give it up to an orphanage and keep quiet.

It was therefore, reported Richard Layton, suspiciously convenient when the girl suddenly fell sick and died of an unspecified illness.

Cromwell was delighted. The scandal of Chicksands Priory was added to his growing list of unholy activity in holy houses and, in due course, presented to the King. Henry, in his turn, was delighted. He closed down the monasteries, taking their wealth for himself, and ennobled Cromwell as the Earl of Essex.

In all the congratulatory back-slapping and redistribution of wealth that was going on, nobody gave much of a thought to the poor novice nun of Chicksands. Where she was buried, or even her name, were forgotten. But the ghost knows, for it is the phantom of this unhappy girl that walks the grounds of Chicksands Priory. Or so goes the best-known version of the tale that circulates around the place.

Unfortunately for the nun story, the ghost was not reported as walking at Chicksands before World War II. It is possible that the old scandal of the novice nun was unearthed to explain the haunting. So what of the ghost herself? The figure of a woman in black had been seen in the closing days of the war and through the later 1940s by RAF personnel at the Chicksands Priory base, but it was not until 1954 that anyone got a good enough look at the ghost to describe her accurately.

The young airman who saw her reported that the ghostly woman was fairly youthful and had a ruddy, freckled face topped by reddish, rather untidy hair. She was dressed in a long black dress with a white collar, perhaps made of lace. The ghost held in her hand a notebook at which she glanced before vanishing as abruptly as she had appeared. The description might fit that of a nun. The long black dress with a white collar might be a robe and wimple, while the notepad might be a small Bible. On the other hand lace would be most unnatural clothing for a nun, who would be more likely to wear a simple cotton collar.

There are other explanations too. Some hold that this is the ghost of a servicewoman from the war who was stationed at Chicksands, others that she is a servant from the days when this was a grand manor. The truth is that nobody really knows who the phantom lady in black might be. The tale of the nun is as good as any, so perhaps it would be best to believe that story.

SHILLINGTON

The village of Shillington stands on the slopes of the chalk hills of southern Bedfordshire, and for years earned wealth from the nearby chalkpits. It is wealth of a very different kind, however, that attracts the ghost of Shillington.

On a ridge towards Pegsdon stands the Knocking Knoll. This curiously shaped mound is, in fact, a prehistoric burial mound. Its exact date is unclear, but about 1500 BC would be about right. On moonlit nights a solitary figure can be seen striding towards the mound. He is tall, muscular and dressed in armour, with a stout sword strapped to his waist. This phantom walks up to the Knocking Knoll and bangs on the side of the mound with a firm hand. He listens carefully, then vanishes.

The haunted Knocking Knoll is just one of several ancient burial mounds on the hills around Shillington.

Local legend has it that this is an ancient king or ruler of great wealth. He is checking to make sure that his vast treasure is still safely buried within the ancient mound. The locals were in little doubt that this formidable figure would interrupt anyone who tried to excavate for any hidden valuables.

In the later 19th century a group

of antiquarians from London heard the stories, but were not put off by the tales of the ghostly guardian. They decided to excavate the mound, and set to work with shovels, picks and great enthusiasm. After many hours of digging, they had found only a few broken bronze trinkets and a skull. They declared that there was no treasure to be had, denouncing the locals as being rural simpletons for believing such a tale.

That very night the ghostly warrior returned. He surveyed the digging in silence, then bending forwards, knocked loudly. Satisfied his treasures were still safe, he turned and vanished.

TODDINGTON

The Bell Inn at Toddington stands facing across the village green to the busy A5120. During rush hours, the main road is so tricky to cross on foot that it almost splits the village into two.

Back in the days when the ghost of the Bell was a real living human, there was no such problem. In the 1850s, the A5120 was the rather more mundane Dunstable Road. It was busy enough for its time with farm carts, passing country folk and the occasional gentry in a carriage, but getting from one side to the other rarely presented a problem.

There were, however, problems aplenty at the Bell. The landlord of the time had a daughter of more than usual prettiness. This was no bad thing, for travelling gentlemen and local farmboys were more inclined to drink their ale and purchase their snacks at a pub with a pretty serving girl than at a pub without one. Unfortunately the girl had the most appalling temper. She was liable to fly into tantrums on the slightest provocation, and at such times customers fled rather than have a tankard of ale upended over them or food thrown in their faces.

The girl's father, of course, knew his daughter and gradually got to recognise the signs that presaged an imminent outbreak of violent temper. Wasting no time, he would bundle the girl into a back room and lock the door. There she would remain until she had vented her anger on pots, pans and other unbreakable objects. An hour or two of mayhem later, and the girl would calm down enough to be released.

But one day the sounds of crashing pans and stamping feet lasted barely ten minutes before an unnatural silence spread through the pub. After a few minutes, the landlord warily opened the door to find his poor daughter dead of a seizure. Perhaps the tantrum had been too much for her.

Ever since then, the Bell has been subjected to occasional outbreaks of ghostly temper tantrums.

Unlike most pubs, which sport a painted sign, the Bell Inn at Toddington has a large bell hanging outside.

Pans will be thrown across the kitchen, pictures jump off the walls and glasses slither along the bars. Strangely, nothing is ever broken nor does any customer find himself drenched with the good, honest ale that the pub still serves. The sudden outbreaks of flying utensils and moving furniture are more a nuisance than a problem.

Perhaps the girl's rage has calmed down over the years that she has been a ghost.

LINSLADE

Quite what it is that has upset the ghost of the Buckingham Arms in Linslade nobody knows. But everybody is agreed that he must be very distressed indeed to indulge in the antics that he does. Not that he is present the entire time. Sometimes months will pass with not a sign of him.

And then, early in the morning, the front gate will unlatch itself and swing open to hang loosely on its hinges. After a few seconds, just long enough for someone to walk up the short front path, loud knocks sound on the door. And the Buckingham Arms is in for a disturbed time.

On such days, the ghost crashes about in the cellar, sounding for all the world as if he is smashing the barrels to pieces – though damage is never done. Or he may run up the stairs with heavy pounding footfalls and seem to dash from room to room opening and slamming doors – though no doors ever seem to move.

It is the opening of the front gate at the Buckingham Arms at Linslade that heralds the approaching ghost.

Who this noisy ghost might be is unknown. Why he crashes around so loudly is utterly obscure. Like all the ghosts of Bedfordshire and Buckinghamshire, he comes to the mortal world and intrudes noisily and dramatically for a while. Then like the other ghosts he goes back to wherever it is he came from – and leaves the good folk of the area to return to their more normal, day to day activities.

STANBRIDGE

Station Road at Stanbridge, just outside Leighton Buzzard, does not lead to a station any longer. In the 1960s Dr Beeching wielded his infamous axe over the railway line that once ran here. But the road remains, and so does the ghost of one forlorn railway passenger.

This is the notorious hitchhiker of Stanbridge, who has been accosting cars and causing upset to their drivers for at least 50 years. It is presumed that the ghost is that of a rail traveller who alighted at Stanbridge and needed a lift to continue his journey to some local destination. He stands by the side of the road dressed in a perfectly respectable country suit of tweeds, flagging down passing motorists.

More than one driver, who has not heard of the phantom's antics, has pulled up beside the road to offer a lift, only to find the man has vanished. This is, perhaps, just as well. Nobody could want to have a ghost in their car. And of course none of the locals will offer a lift to anyone hitchhiking on Station Road in case it is the ghost – so any genuine hitchhikers will be severely out of luck.

LUTON

Luton is a prosperous and thriving town with solid industrial backbone. There is an airport, with all the associated aeronautical activities that such an establishment brings, and the town has generations-old links to the Vauxhall car and truck firm. As London satellite towns go, Luton is about as industrial as they get.

It is all the more surprising, therefore, that this great manufacturing complex and bustling town gained its initial boost and prosperity from objects as humble as straw hats. It was the weaving of straw from Bedfordshire fields into hats that gave Luton its start in industry during the 17th century. Most farmers were accustomed to making their own hats from straw in their own fields, but the nimble-fingered folk of Luton were soon producing hats better and cheaper – and so they won a reputation as a solid workforce that the town never lost.

Unfortunately, some of the citizens of Luton were nimble-fingered in other ways. Travellers passing through on their way to and from London often stopped off in Luton's inns and taverns. All too often, or so it seemed to the travellers, they left with rather less money than they had when they arrived. Tolerating thieving was not a good reputation for a town to have, especially one that hoped to make a good honest living selling food and drink to the travellers.

So the town authorities set up beside the main road on Galley Hill, right on the skyline where it could be seen for miles, a gibbet. And on that gibbet they hung the bodies of any local folk sent to the scaffold for theft or violence. Not content with this grim landmark, the Luton magistrates ordered that the bodies of executed criminals should be soaked in tar for three days before being bound in chains and hoisted onto the gibbet. This ensured that the bodies would swing in the wind for months before they rotted and, or so the Luton magistrates believed, serve as an effective deterrent to any would be thieves. At least, the honest tradesmen hoped, it would persuade travellers that the town took law and order seriously, so that trade would return and Luton could continue to enjoy a prosperous living.

For some years in the early 18th century the gibbet did its gruesome business well enough. Malefactors were hanged, soaked in tar and dangled in chains; travellers trusted Luton's magistrates to enforce the law, and the citizens of Luton did a roaring trade. Only the criminals suffered, and nobody much cared about their views.

Then one night a fierce storm swept down on Luton. There was not much rain, but wind and lightning there was in plenty. Set high on Galley Hill, the gibbet attracted the lightning. One bolt hit the gibbet with a shattering crack and set it alight. The tarred bodies flared fiercely while the stout timber crackled and blazed. Before long a towering pillar of flames was leaping skywards from Galley Hill. The good folk of Luton gazed in awe at the fire. They soon had reason to fear.

Something was seen dancing around the flames of that awful pyre. As the townspeople watched, the 'something' became rather more definite in shape

For decades the gibbet outside Luton was an arresting sight for travellers
heading north from London.

and emerged as a huge, black dog, which pranced around the flames for hours until the fire died down to a pile of black embers. Then the apparition howled with a terrifyingly piercing voice, leapt on to the ashes and vanished.

Nobody was certain what the strange creature had been, but everyone was convinced it was evil. Why else would it delight so in the burning bodies of wicked men? At odd intervals after that terrible night, the dog would return to Galley Hill. Travellers would find themselves confronted by the most enormous black hound, some said it was as big as a pony. With glowing red eyes and a sinister growl, the dog would block the road. Wise travellers turned back, unwise travellers were not heard of again.

That, at least, is the story told about the black hound of Galley Hill. That a gibbet stood on the hill until the later 18th century is without question. And the phantom hound is a reasonably well-known ghost in Luton.

But the black hound that blocks roads is not unique to Luton, nor to Galley Hill, but is familiar in many parts of England. He is known most often as Black Shuck, and is generally reckoned to be the Devil's dog. Wherever he is seen, Black Shuck patrols roads and paths. He is huge and jet-black in colour. Often he has glowing eyes of an unnaturally round shape and long, sharp claws. Sometimes Black Shuck will trot past the human who sees him, at other times he will fix the human with a baleful stare that can bring only bad luck. And just occasionally he will block the road or path so that none may pass.

Black Shuck is a truly terrifying phantom. He may, indeed, be the Devil's dog. But he may also be an older spectre than that. Some folklorists have noted that Black Shuck is usually reported as being seen near prehistoric monuments or on roads that have not changed their route since pre-Roman days. They suggest that he may be some pagan god or spirit that has somehow managed to survive the Christianisation of these islands.

Whatever the Black Shuck may in reality be, one thing is certain. Those who walk up Galley Hill are well advised to avoid him.

The Cork and Bull pub in Luton marks one end of a route followed by a mysterious Grey Lady.

* * *

Nothing like as terrifying as the hell hound of Galley Hill is the ghost that flits around the town centre between Cumberland Street and St Mary's Road. Those who have seen her, and there are many, say this ghost is of an elderly woman dressed in a grey dress of Victorian styling. The Grey Lady of Luton, as she is dubbed on the occasions when she features in the local press, seems to walk the area bounded by St Mary's church on the one hand and the Cork and Bull pub on the other.

There could not be two more different buildings. St Mary's is one of the largest churches in England. Considering it was built in the 13th and 14th centuries, before Luton gained wealth as a straw hat manufacturing centre, this was an impressive achievement for an otherwise unremarkable little market town. The exterior has a striking black and white design built up out of white limestone blocks and black-knapped flint. The interior preserves much of the elaborate work destroyed during the Reformation elsewhere. The Wenlock Chapel is two storeys tall while the chantry chapel of Richard Barnard, dating from 1477, has one of the most ornate vaults in Europe.

The Cork and Bull, by contrast, is a plain, modern building with, some think, little architectural merit and much neon lighting. There can be no missing the pub, nor the ghost. She is one of those phantoms that appear to be very real and solid. Such ghosts are not at all unusual and make up the majority of spectres that are reported. Artists and film-makers may favour semi-transparent figures that hover some inches above the ground, but ghosts are not generally like that. The majority of ghosts appear as real and solid as do you. Very often they are mistaken for a real person by those who see them.

A few years ago the Grey Lady was likewise taken for a living human by a new, young staff member at one of the shops along

The Black Hound of Luton resulted from a dramatic conflagration on Galley Hill.

her route. Thinking the elderly lady in the long dress was pausing to consider a purchase, the girl asked if she wanted help with anything. The phantom just stared straight through her and moved on.

Why the Grey Lady of Luton should wander forever between these two very different places is unclear. In Victorian times, when she would have been alive, the site now covered by the Cork and Bull was a tavern. Some believe that she lived in the pub, or one of the properties nearby, and died here in somewhat unusual circumstances, but then such things are often said to try to explain why ghosts walk. In truth, little is known about the Grey Lady, except that she promenades from the church to the pub and back again on some endless quest known only to herself.

KENSWORTH

The church of St Mary the Virgin at Kensworth is unusual in a number of ways. Not structurally, however, as it is unremarkable, although charming.

The most obvious way in which it is odd is its position. It stands on a steeply sloping, south-facing chalk hill a good half mile away from the village of Kensworth. The walk to and from the church is made more strenuous by the fact that a steep, deep valley lies between the two. Why the good folk of Kensworth should have chosen to build their place of worship there, not in the village, is unknown. Clearly there was something about the site that meant the church had to go here, for why else would the people burden themselves with a strenuous hill walk every Sunday?

From the rear of the churchyard a stile gives access to a broad, grassy field that sweeps up over the chalk hill towards a distant wood. And it is this field that really marks Kensworth church out from so many others in Bedfordshire. There are two ghosts in the field. Both walk towards the church, but only one of them actually gets there.

The ghost that remains in the field is that of an old woman who wears a most peculiar hat. It is said to be black, with a low crown surrounded by a brim

The church at Kensworth attracts two ghosts, only one of which reaches it.

that has four corners. Such hats were not common even when fashionable back in the 18th century, when most folk favoured the three-cornered, or tricorn, hat. This ghost walks down the path from the woods, but when she reaches the stile in to the churchyard she stops abruptly and waves a fist at the church.

It is said that she is a witch who is forbidden entrance into the holy precincts and so eternally displays her anger at God's acre.

The second phantom does make her way into the churchyard, and she is altogether more disturbing than the woman in black. This ghost is of a young milkmaid dressed in a garment of homespun cloth made to a rural cut that could date her to almost any period of the 17th to early 20th centuries. Across her shoulders she carries a yoke from which dangle two pails of milk. Presumably she is returning from the grasslands of the chalk hills where she had been milking cows or ewes grazing the lush pasture.

The stile into the churchyard of St Mary the Virgin at Kensworth, which proves to be an insurmountable obstacle to one of the ghosts.

The most striking thing about this phantom is, however, that she lacks a head. The neck of the ghost has been sliced clean through. There are no gory bloodstains, nor any sign of an injury that may have deprived the poor girl of her head, but gone it is.

This would appear to be one of those instances where a most startling ghost has no real story to explain it. Some say that she is a girl who was waylaid and murdered on the path, but there are no records of any such crime. Others say that she was killed accidentally by one of the steam-driven farm machines of the early 19th century. Again, no records of such a gruesome accident can be found. A third tale has the girl dying a quite natural death, but having her head sliced off after death by a crazed lover who sought to keep her with him for ever.

None of these stories can be proved to be untrue, but none has any evidence to support it. And yet the headless milkmaid persistently walks her route down from the hills and into the churchyard. The unanswered question is why?

STUDHAM

S tudham is one of those villages that nobody goes to, unless they mean to go there. It is not on the way to anywhere else and the roads around it are clearly enough signposted so that few will get lost and stumble there by accident.

But this is no out of the way backwater. Studham's church of St Mary dates from the 13th century, and was greatly enhanced two centuries later by the famous Sir Reginald Bray, who had already been responsible for St George's Chapel in Windsor and went on to build Henry VII's chapel in Westminster Abbey. His work at Studham is not as famous as his other creations, perhaps because it is in this quiet, rural village, but it is no less beautiful.

The good folk of Studham have maintained the tradition of fine building. When they were in need of a war memorial they ignored the practice of their fellows who erected crosses or statues and instead opted for an idiosyncratic clock tower on the edge of the common that sweeps down from the Dunstable Downs. Surrounded by a tiny, hedged garden, the clock tower greets visitors to the village with elegance and the correct time. For those who linger to read the inscription it has a rather unusual war casualty to record. Along with the brave men who went off to serve King

The unusual war memorial at Studham.

and Country and lose their lives in foreign fields is one Miss Olive May Hart who died of shock aged just 22 when caught in a Zeppelin raid.

It is the common beyond the clock tower that is haunted. Again, even when dealing with ghosts, Studham avoids the humdrum. This phantom is of a short, bearded man dressed in a neat blue suit and tall-crowned hat. He will come up to walkers on the common as if he wants to ask a question. Far from vanishing before speaking, as other ghosts are prone to do, the ghost of Studham Common asks his question clearly and distinctly. Unfortunately the man is not from England for the question he asks is in some foreign language that none who have heard it can understand. Realising that he cannot make himself understood, the ghost mutters in exasperation – and then vanishes.

•North Buckinghamshire•

WOUGHTON ON THE GREEN

These days Woughton on the Green is one of the uniform suburbs of Milton Keynes, that experimental example of 1960s new town planning. In the past forty or so years, it has been engulfed in a sea of sweeping boulevards, concrete structures and modern architecture.

But it was not always this way. Woughton on the Green is one of the oldest villages in Buckinghamshire, being mentioned in the Domesday Book, and occupied a prominent position on the banks of the River Ouzel. Remnants of past days remain, the church being medieval and both Woughton House and the Olde Swan inn dating back centuries. All three of these buildings face The Green, itself a scheduled ancient monument, and it is here that the phantom of Woughton on the Green lurks.

The new cul-de-sac off the haunted lane at Woughton on the Green has an appropriate name.

The ghost in question is usually only glimpsed. Mounted on a dark horse, the man is dressed in dark clothes and wears a tricorn hat. Few see more than that, as the ghost rides out of sight behind a hedge or round a corner. Some people have got a better view, including one who saw the phantom in the mid-1980s. This witness described the man as being dressed in a cloak over a fancy waistcoat with thigh high top boots of black leather.

Clearly the phantom dates back to the 18th century, but who is he?

The locals at Woughton on the Green have few doubts. Their ghost is the spirit of none other than the famous highwayman Dick Turpin. Although the mysterious rider is rarely seen clearly enough to be certain, the identification is more than likely. Watling Street, now better known as the A5, runs close to the village on its way from London to Chester. The rich merchants who used the road made easy pickings for men such as Turpin, and he is known to have held up more than one coach on this route.

Also certain is the fact that the notorious highwayman came to Woughton on the Green at least once. Turpin was planning a particularly daring robbery and was reasonably certain that he would quickly be pursued by armed guards. Before setting out on his job, he came to the village and visited the inn, where the blacksmith then plied his trade.

Turpin paid the burly smith handsomely for a rather unusual task. He instructed that his horse's shoes should all be removed and replaced, but demanded that the new ones should be put on backwards. Only after the robbery had taken place did the purpose of this strange request become clear. As Turpin galloped off, his horse left hoofprints leading towards the crime scene, not away from it. The baffled pursuers soon gave up the chase and the highwayman got clean away. Turpin's ghost is also said to frequent Trap's Hill at Loughton, three miles to the west, where the hold-up actually happened.

Dick Turpin is a strange character. He is said to haunt several places around England and is mentioned in folklore at locations he almost certainly never visited. He is often spoken of as if he were a daring, dashing hero who robbed the unworthy rich to give money to the poor.

Such an image of highwaymen had some elements of truth. Several of the first 'gentlemen of the road' were well-born cavaliers who had lost their wealth when Charles I was defeated in the Civil War of the 1640s. Riding around on their magnificent chargers and dressed in beautifully tailored clothes of finest cloth, these men were clearly a cut above the average robber. They treated their victims with gallantry and politeness, rarely bothering to relieve a poor farmer of his pennies. Before long many other villains aspired to the status that went with being a highwayman. If they could afford the clothes and the horse, they took to the road to ape the manners of the gentry and earn the admiration of criminal colleagues.

By the time Dick Turpin became a highwayman, however, they were a vanishing breed. The authorities had developed mounted patrols and better methods of gaining information. It was becoming too dangerous to rob travellers on the king's highway. Turpin was one of the last men to adopt the lifestyle, and it is on this that his fame largely rests. He had been a burglar and cattle thief for some years before, in July 1735, he donned the fine clothes and manners of the highwayman and took to the road. After a career of two years robbing coaches and travellers on the main roads leading out of London, Turpin retired to Yorkshire and assumed the name of John Palmer.

In 1738 Turpin visited Welton in Yorkshire and, apparently for sport, shot a cockerel in the street. The bird's owner demanded payment, but 'Palmer' merely threatened him. The man had the malefactor arrested. By chance Turpin's old schoolmaster happened to see a letter sent by 'Palmer' and recognised the handwriting. Turpin was rapidly identified and on 7th April 1739 was executed. True to his criminal profession, Turpin ordered a new set of fashionable clothes for the event and spent his time entertaining friends and celebrities in his cell. He died bravely, without a single sign of fear.

A scene played out all too often on the roads around
Woughton on the Green when Dick Turpin was at large.

The age of the highwayman was over, except in Woughton on the Green where Turpin's galloping ghost still has the power to alarm travellers.

BUCKINGHAM

In 1725 a great fire swept through the town of Buckingham. Nearly every house in the town was gutted, and the whole area reduced to a charred ruin. Few people were killed, however, and the good citizens of Buckingham moved back to rebuild their town on a new and much grander scale. Gone were the old wooden houses, to be replaced with fine brick structures in the very latest Georgian style. It is this new town that largely survives to greet visitors.

The haunted Castle House at Buckingham, which originated in the 15th century, was built to provide more comfortable lodgings for visiting gentry than were available in the ancient castle. It is now a private house and is not open to the public.

Perhaps the most important building to be destroyed in the fire was Buckingham Castle. The fortification dated back to AD 888 when Alfred the Great, King of Wessex, built an earth and timber fortress here to block a crossing point over the River Great Ouse to the armies of marauding Vikings that then plagued England. Most of the castle that burned down was of later, medieval date. The stones were later reused to build the castle-like prison, now the tourist information centre and council offices, that stands on the site today.

Not far from the castle was one house that did survive the conflagration. It was the comfortable dwelling in West Street that went by the name of Castle House. This was begun in the 15th century, though it has been much altered since, to provide more fashionable lodgings and accommodation for the gentry and notables who visited Buckingham and who would have found the old castle with its fortifications too cold and draughty.

The most famous of the guests to stay in Castle House was Catherine of Aragon, the first wife of Henry VIII. It is this sad queen whose stay led, indirectly, to the haunting of the house. The unhappy Queen Catherine came to Buckingham in the later 1520s when her husband was trying to find grounds to divorce her. Henry was, by this time, infatuated with Anne Boleyn who was much younger and prettier than Catherine and who seemed to offer a better prospect of providing a son and heir. Buckingham was deemed far enough away from London for Catherine to be kept out of Henry's way, but close enough to allow her and her lawyers to play a role in the divorce proceedings.

Among Catherine's household was a priest by the name of Thomas. This Father Thomas not only administered mass and confession to Catherine, but also played a key role in smuggling messages to her relatives in Europe. He would slip away, sometimes for weeks, then return just as mysteriously. One day this priest vanished, but never again reappeared. What had happened to him remained unclear until the house was undergoing renovations in 1908.

A small chamber was found hidden beneath the floors of the upper storeys, above the Great Parlour. Inside this tiny room was the skeleton of a man accompanied by the crucifix, rosary and other belongings of a Tudor priest. Had the man proved too efficient a servant of the Queen and been killed by the King? Or had he betrayed Catherine and been disposed of on her orders? Or was his death a tragic accident? There is no way of knowing.

What is clear, however, is that the priest does not seem to approve of having been discovered. Ever since the body was found the dark robed figure of a priest has been spotted hurrying up the stairs and along the corridor towards the hidden chamber. He is seen most often in late afternoon or early evening. A clue, perhaps, to the time of the priest's death.

SWANBOURNE

The charming village of Swanbourne provides, for many, the essence of rural Buckinghamshire. The old Manor House has stone mullioned windows, scarcely having changed since it was built in the 16th century. The nearby cottages of Smithfield Close date back as far and form a picturesque scene of thatch and low eaves. Everything clusters around the main village street, which runs past both the manor and the church. It is here, too, that the ghost is seen.

The main street at Swanbourne. It is here that the Green Lady is seen most often.

The phantom of Swanbourne is an elegant lady dressed all in green, walking quietly towards the church of St Swithun with her head bowed and hands clasped. There is no doubt about the identity of this Green Lady for the ghost was first seen only a few weeks after the lady's death and was instantly recognised by several villagers who had known her in life.

The ghost is that of Elizabeth Adams, wife of Thomas Adams. The Adams family has been connected with Swanbourne for generations. Only the Fremantles, one of whom fought alongside Nelson at Trafalgar, can rival the Adams family for the length of time spent in and around the village.

This particular Adams had a sad and tragic life. She married into the family when quite young, bearing the handsome Thomas four children. Everything seemed set fair, but in October 1627 disaster struck. Thomas was waylaid by thieves who took not only his valuables and money, but also his life. The widow Elizabeth never really recovered from the shock of hearing of his death. She was devoted to her children and brought them up in the village as well as anyone could hope, but the joy had gone from her life. Every evening she would be seen walking towards the church to pay her respects at the tomb of her beloved husband.

Gradually poor Elizabeth faded away. As her children grew older, she seemed to lose the will to live. Finally, she slipped away quietly in her sleep and her body was brought to St Swithun's to lie alongside her husband for eternity. And then her ghost began to be seen, following the route she had taken every evening in life.

And she takes it still.

MIDDLE CLAYDON

One ghost that haunts the magnificent National Trust property of Claydon House, to the west of Winslow, is simply wandering around his old home. Those who have seen him report that he is not in the least bit frightening. They may be startled to see a one-armed man clad in old fashioned clothes pottering about, but that is all.

This ghost came to haunt Claydon House in a most unusual and dramatic fashion. He is Sir Edmund Verney, one time Member of Parliament and noted soldier. In the troubled years leading up to the English Civil War, Sir Edmund held the prestigious post of Standard Bearer to the King. The post gave him high precedence at court, but in the long years of peace involved nothing more arduous than carrying the royal banner on ceremonial occasions. He was a Puritan by religion and consistently supported the democratic rights of Parliament over the autocratic powers of the monarch.

Nevertheless, when the Civil War did break out, Sir Edmund unhesitatingly sided with the King. As he told his friend the Earl of Clarendon: 'I do not like the quarrel and do heartily wish that the King would yield and consent to what Parliament desires. My conscience is only concerned with honour and gratitude to follow my master. I have eaten his bread and served him near thirty years, and will not do so base a thing as to forsake him now.'

So Sir Edmund Verney got out the royal battle standard, made sure it was in good repair and carried it to Nottingham where King Charles performed the ceremony of raising the standard and called on all loyal Britons to rally to his cause. Sir Edmund was accompanied by an aged servant named Jason, who swore to follow wherever he led.

After some months of negotiation, manoeuvre and general time wasting, the King's army met that of Parliament at Edgehill in Warwickshire in October 1642. The battle, fought between large numbers of poorly trained amateur soldiers, was a confused affair. At one point a Parliamentarian cavalry attack surged into the very centre of the Royalist line. The Roundheads headed for the royal standard, although the King himself was in another part of the fray. A group of a dozen troopers surrounded Sir Edmund and Jason and demanded that Sir Edmund surrender and hand over the flag.

Sir Edmund refused. 'My life is my own,' he declared. 'But this standard is the King's and I cannot surrender it.' Jason died first, then Sir Edmund. But the troopers could not prise Sir Edmund's fingers from the staff he held so tightly. Instead they hacked off his arm and rode away with their prize.

At this point, a party of Royalist cavalry were returning to the battle after a successful charge of their own. One of the boys saw the banner being taken off.

The main gates to Claydon House, scene of a ghostly reminder of the English Civil War.

'Captain Smith,' he yelled, 'they are taking away the standard.' Captain Smith and his men put their spurs to their horses, overwhelmed the Roundheads and retrieved the royal standard. When the flag was brought back to the King, the distraught monarch saw the severed arm that still gripped the flagpole. One of the fingers wore the distinctive gold ring carrying a miniature portrait of the King that Sir Edmund had worn into battle.

After the battle had ended in stalemate, Sir Edmund's lifeless fingers were at last eased away from the standard. The severed limb was taken back to Claydon House and given a decent burial, no sign of the rest of the body being found amid the carnage of the battlefield.

And then the ghost began to walk. Sir Edmund returned to his home dressed not in the armour in which he had died, but in the fashionable clothes of a gentleman of the mid-17th century. He is seen most often on or near the staircase. The more gruesome accounts maintain that he walks with blood dripping from the severed stump of his right arm, but none of the witnesses that have seen him recently recount this detail. Some agree the arm is missing, but none report such a hideous detail as dripping blood.

There is said to be another ghost at Claydon House, though she does not seem to appear as often as the phantom of Sir Edmund. This is the gentle Grey Lady who frequents the lounge known as the Rose Room – standing in the room momentarily before fading from view. Whenever she is seen a feeling of tranquillity and charm in the air is described.

She is generally thought to be Florence Nightingale, whose sister Parthenope was married to Sir Harry Verney in the later 19th century. Nightingale was famous in her day as the Lady with the Lamp, having tirelessly cared for the wounded soldiers of the Crimean War even to the point of walking the wards late at night to see if any soldier needed comfort or support. She later became involved with transforming the status and training of nurses in Britain and abroad. It was largely through the efforts of Florence Nightingale that nurses earned the place in the hearts of millions that they hold today.

Although Florence Nightingale's home was in Hampshire, she often visited her sister and spent many months living at Claydon House. Since the Grey Lady was seen only after her death in 1910 it was natural for the phantom to be identified with her, though in truth the shrouded figure has been viewed only indistinctly and the identification cannot be certain.

WHITCHURCH

Whitchurch is a pretty village, strung out along the A413 north of Aylesbury. The White Swan pub looks out over the main road, while the ancient church is set back to the north. But it is not Whitchurch itself that is haunted; the grand house nearby has that honour.

Creslow Manor dates back to around 1120 and lies just north-east of the village. The manor was first owned by the Knights Templar, then transferred to the Hospitallers – both stern, religious brotherhoods of fighting monks dedicated to winning and defending with the sword the holy places connected to the life of Jesus Christ. They had no time for fripperies or the secular vanities. So they would probably disapprove most strongly of the ghost that now haunts their ancient home.

After the Reformation saw the Hospitallars, and other monastic orders, stripped of their wealth and lands, Creslow Manor was seized by the Crown. The King leased the manor and lands out to whoever could afford the rent, and in the 17th century that was the Clifford family.

Sir Thomas Clifford was far and away the most famous and powerful Clifford of his time. In 1665, at the age of 35, he was knighted by Charles II, newly restored to his throne after the upheavals of the Civil War. By 1668 he had risen to be Treasurer to the King and two years later was Secretary of State and was raised to the peerage as Baron Clifford of Chudleigh. He was also a nobleman of the Holy Roman Empire, having inherited a grand, if impoverished title, from his mother. Clifford was, by this time, the most powerful man in government, after the King, and one of only three men in England who knew the full details of the secret Treaty of Dover with the French.

Then, in 1673, the public were seriously alarmed by reports of a foreign conspiracy of Catholics aimed at deposing the popular Charles II in favour of his considerably less popular, and very Catholic, brother James. Charles was forced to dismiss his Catholic ministers, and so Baron Clifford of Chudleigh retired to spend more time with his family. The most important member of his family was his wife, Lady Rosamund. For some years the Baron had left her to wander alone around the various estates he held, to find her own entertainment while he played politics. Now, happily reunited, the couple lived out their short final years.

It is the phantom of Lady Rosamund that returns, night after night, to haunt the upstairs of Creslow Manor. She is never seen, but the sound of her light footsteps and the distinct rustling of her heavy silk dress is heard often as if the lady herself is walking gently around the rooms of her old home. It is, a witness said, just as if somebody has walked up behind you, but when you turn there is nobody there.

In 1858 the haunted chamber of Creslow Manor became suddenly famous when the High Sheriff of Buckingham, no less, volunteered to stay in the room.

Declaring that he had no fear of any woman, alive or dead, the High Sheriff retired, armed with a box of matches, a brace of pistols and a sword. He locked the door behind him and barricaded the windows.

Next morning the High Sheriff failed to appear at breakfast. The servants reported that the jug of water left outside his door for his use was untouched. Everyone was beginning to fear the worst and wondering if they should break the door down, when the missing man strolled in the front door. He had, he said, been out for a long walk.

At around 2 am the High Sheriff had heard the soft tread of a lady's footsteps approaching his door along the silent corridor. He was alarmed when the footsteps continued through the locked door into his chamber, accompanied by the sound of rustling silk. The noises stopped for a few seconds, as if the invisible woman had halted. Then they began again, retreating back through the locked door and along the corridor. Thoroughly frightened, the man had hurriedly unlocked his door and fled into the night.

ICKNIELD WAY

The Icknield Way can lay claim to being the oldest road in Buckinghamshire, so it is surely right that it should also claim to be the haunt of the oldest ghost in the county.

The road runs from the North Sea coast beside the Wash at Thornham, sweeping south around the low fens to join the high ground and then run southwest to cross the Thames and climb up to the high ground of Salisbury Plain. The road was certainly in use by around 3000 BC, but was probably at its busiest from around 2000 BC to the Roman Conquest in the first century AD. It linked the rich grain fields and productive flint mines of East Anglia to the heavily populated areas of the South West.

When the Romans conquered southern Britain their military needs were quite different from those served by the economic trade routes of the native Celts. They needed a straight road along which the legions could march from the military ports in Kent, through the provincial capital of London and on to the military frontier posts of Chester and York. For Buckinghamshire, that meant a road was built running north-west towards Chester. The old and new roads crossed near Ivinghoe Beacon – it was to prove to be a fatal junction.

In AD 60 the Romans broke their agreement with the Iceni tribe of East Anglia. The tribal kingdom's status as an ally of Rome was revoked and the lands annexed. Queen Boadicea objected, but was flogged and her daughters raped, while the noblemen were robbed of their wealth and harsh new taxes were imposed on the ordinary Iceni. For several months it appeared that the Romans had cowed resistance, but the Iceni were merely laying their plans.

In AD 61, the Iceni rose in revolt, led by Boadicea. Other tribal kingdoms joined the revolt, which flashed across southern Britain with a ferocity that caught the Romans by surprise. Colchester went up in flames, so did St Albans

---

Queen Boadicea drove her chariot down the Icknield Way on her march to a fatal encounter with the Romans.

and London. Within days the three largest Roman cities in Britain were smoking ruins and over 50,000 citizens were dead. British reinforcements poured along the Icknield Way to join Boadicea as she marched up the new Roman Watling Street to confront the main Roman army. Led by Governor Suetonius Paulinus, the Roman army had been in North Wales dealing with some rebellious druids.

The two armies met somewhere near the junction of the Icknield Way and Watling Street, though the site is now lost. The battle was a climactic affair, but Roman discipline triumphed over British dash and courage.

Most of the British army died that day, or in the pursuit that followed. Thereafter the Romans were rather more careful in how they treated the British, preferring compromise and honouring promises to having to face another rebellion.

Boadicea herself took poison rather than be captured and, according to tradition, was buried just outside the walls of London under what is now King's Cross Station. But her ghost lives on. She has been seen several times riding in her war chariot down the Icknield Way towards the site of her final battle. As befits a sovereign queen of a Celtic people, she is dressed in her finest jewellery and in striking clothes of bright colours. Perhaps surprisingly she does not gallop along the old road, but trots along as if she has all the time in the world. These days, of course, she does.

•South Buckinghamshire•

HADDENHAM

The haunting at Haddenham made English legal history. After all, it is not very often that a ghost features at a murder trial. The grim story began innocently enough at dawn on a summer morning in 1848. A farmer by the name of Powell left his home in Haddenham with a cart loaded down with produce from his acres to take to market in Thame. His wife, as so often before, waved him goodbye before returning to her children and her chores around the farm. Powell was seen to have a successful day in Thame, selling his produce at good prices well before the market wound down in the late afternoon. Then he clambered back on to his cart, urged his horse into a gentle trot and set off up the road towards Haddenham. He never got there.

Mrs Powell waited until long after dark before, fraught with worry, she roused her neighbours. A group of men set off down the road towards Thame. A short distance outside the village they came across Farmer Powell's cart, but of him there was no sign. When daylight came, a search was carried out but nothing was to be found.

Two days later the mystery was as impenetrable as ever. But then Mrs Powell was shocked to see her husband stagger in through the entrance to the farmyard. He was clutching his chest in obvious agony and pointing desperately up the road towards Thame. Strange gurgling noises came from his throat as his wife rushed towards him. And then he vanished into thin air. Mrs Powell fainted.

When she came to, the poor woman convinced herself that she had been dreaming. Still upset, however, she set off along the Thame road. Just beyond the spot where the road forded a small stream she saw her husband again. As before, he was gripping his chest and making horrific noises. This time he was

58

The stretch of road outside Haddenham where the ghostly farmer is most often seen.

pointing at the narrow stream, little more than a ditch, that cut across the road. Then he again vanished.

Now convinced that she was not imagining things, Mrs Powell raced back to Haddenham and again roused her neighbours. She insisted that they search the stream, and this time they found the body of Farmer Powell hidden among the tangled water plants some way downstream. The body showed obvious signs of a fight, but death had been caused by a massive blow to the chest by a heavy blacksmith's hammer, which was still embedded in the crushed ribs of the dead man.

The authorities were called and it did not take long to piece together what had happened. A blacksmith, and known petty thief, named Taylor had suddenly come into some money which he was spending freely in the taverns and, significantly, had also bought a hammer to replace one that he had 'lost'. He had seen Powell pocketing a small fortune in silver at the market before setting off home alone. Taylor and a colleague named Smith had followed him and, when the road was empty of other travellers, pounced. Powell had put up a fight, which was brutally ended by Taylor with his hammer.

The trial took place a few weeks later, not that there was any real doubt about the verdict. Taylor and Smith were duly found guilty and taken out to be hanged.

But that was not the end of this tragic affair, though the law had now run its course. For the ghost continued to return to the Thame road – and it lurks there still. It is not a pleasant spectre to encounter. The hideous wounds to the body are all too obvious as blood pours from the chest, and the distressing gurgles and gasps can be heard as the man seems to struggle for breath. He staggers along the road near the small stream, pointing desperately towards the scene of the crime that cost his life. Those that have seen this ghost generally wish they had not.

Much less terrifying are the gentle phantoms that lurk a mile or so to the north. Standing on the banks of the River Thame lie the scattered ruins of Notley Abbey. There is not much to see these days, though in the medieval period this was one of the leading religious houses in Buckinghamshire. As might be expected the ruins are said to be haunted by monks. Walking singly or in procession, the cowled figures drift gently across the water meadows that now spread across the site of their old home. Of the ghosts around Haddenham, there can be no doubt that these are the ones it is better to encounter.

One of the ghostly monks of Notley Abbey.

ELLESBOROUGH

The church of St Peter and St Paul stands near the summit of Church Hill on the western edge of the little village of Ellesborough. It is a charming building, dating back to medieval times, that has managed to preserve much of its character through the centuries.

The ghost that is seen here originated in the early days of the church, when knights in armour roamed the land. It is all the more curious, therefore, that the phantom was not reported before World War II, being first known to have walked during those dark days when Britain feared imminent German invasion and church bells were silenced so that they could be used to issue the news of attack.

The church of St Peter and St Paul in Ellesborough has a persistent ghost.

The church organist was alone in the cool interior practising for the Sunday service when he heard the door open and close. Thinking some parishioner had entered on an errand, the man turned around and was surprised to see a tall man dressed in very strange clothes, later identified as being those of the 14th century gentry. The man walked slowly across the nave to the far wall. When the organist called out to him, the man ignored him, but stepped behind a pillar.

When he did not reappear, the organist left his stool and went to investigate. There was nobody behind the pillar and the church was empty. At the time the organist put the sighting down to some prankster in fancy dress. It was only when the ghost was seen on subsequent occasions that it was realised that this was the first sighting of a rather persistent phantom.

Since his first appearance in the 1940s, the tall ghost in medieval costume has been a fairly frequent visitor to the church. He appears only when the building is almost empty, apparently not liking a full congregation or packed wedding service, and it has been noticed that he usually vanishes at a particular spot while staring at the wall.

The ghostly gentleman of Ellesborough wears clothes of the 14th century.

The only feature on the wall is a tablet dedicated to the deceased of the Hawtrey family. Since the family members did not live and die until long after the 14th century, it is not entirely clear what interest the ghost may have in the memorial. Perhaps he is searching for some long vanished feature of the church. The Reformation saw many paintings, statues and tombs smashed to pieces if they were considered idolatrous by the Puritans. Was this place once home to the tomb of this enigmatic ghost? If so, why did he start to walk only in the mid-20th century?

Unless the ghost himself gives any answers, it seems this visitor to the church of St Peter and St Paul, and his purpose, will remain shrouded in mystery.

ST LEONARDS

The little village of St Leonards lies between Wendover and Berkhamsted and has long been something of a quiet backwater. The great affairs of state have, generally, passed the village by as effectively as have the main roads and railways.

Just south of the village lies Dundridge Manor, and it was the very quiet of the area that attracted the village's most famous inhabitant to the house. This was Margaret de la Pole, Countess of Salisbury, who came to St Leonards seeking nothing more than a quiet retirement. As events turned out she was to suffer a death as tragic and bloody as her life had been.

She was born to apparent luxury and gentility as the daughter of George, Duke of Clarence, the brother of Edward IV. When still a girl, she lost her father in mysterious circumstance. He was caught plotting to seize political office and lucrative government posts by underhand moves. Although the details of these charges were vague, they were serious enough for him to be held under arrest until he could make peace with his brother. After some weeks of suspense, the King forgave Clarence. But then Clarence was found drowned in a barrel of malmsey wine. It was a strange death, even for a notorious drinker such as the Duke, and it was widely rumoured that he had been killed on the orders of his brother.

Young Margaret soon married Richard de la Pole, brother of John de la Pole, the Duke of Suffolk. Again life seemed set fair for Margaret, but again tragedy struck. After the death of Edward IV, the crown was seized by his brother Richard III. As his own son had died, Richard designated his cousin Duke John as his heir. When Richard was killed in battle in 1485, Duke John inherited the claim to the throne granted by Richard. Two years later he joined a rebellion against the new king, Henry VII, and was killed in battle.

Unsurprisingly, but apparently without any reason, John's young brother Richard came under suspicion of having been involved in the rebellion. With his brother's death, Richard now had a claim to the throne, whether he wanted it or not. He did not want it, as he made clear time and again. Life in England, however, became difficult and unpleasant so Richard and Margaret moved to

France. Even there, the couple could find no rest. King Louis of France went to war with England and in 1512 organised an army of mercenaries to support the claims of 'King Richard IV'. The proposed invasion never came to anything, and the hapless couple now moved to Italy, along with their only son. This boy, Reginald, entered the church as a priest.

In 1525 Richard died in Italy, and Countess Margaret journeyed home to England. She had, naturally enough, had more than enough of politics, intrigue and powergames. So she retired to St Leonards to find peace and repose in her final years. Unfortunately for her, the new King of England was the notoriously suspicious Henry VIII. He did not like the fact that Countess Margaret had royal blood in her veins that was rather closer to the throne than his own, nor had he forgiven her for the actions of her in-laws. In particular he hated the fact that young Reginald de la Pole was now a cardinal of the Church in Rome and was preaching against Henry's divorce of his queen, Catherine of Aragon.

King Henry VIII who, in vengeful mood, ordered the execution that was to lead to the haunting at St Leonards by the tranquil ghost of Margaret de la Pole.

In 1539 Henry organised trumped up charges against Margaret. She was arrested and dragged to the Tower of London for trial and then for execution. When the elderly countess was led out on to Tower Green to face the axeman, she waited for a suitable opportunity then loudly proclaimed her innocence and fled. Pursued by guards and the executioner, Countess Margaret had almost reached the open gates of the Tower when she was brought down. Putting his foot on her chest, the axeman hacked off her head with a single blow. It was a savage and bloody end to a tragic life.

But it was not the end of Countess Margaret. She had evidently enjoyed her time in St Leonards and her ghost soon returned to the only place she had ever known peace and tranquillity. She is seen most often in the summer months wandering in the grounds of Dundridge Manor and nearby fields or lanes. With her graceful step and smiling face, the ghost seems to be at peace. After such a life of tragedy, it is to be hoped that Countess Margaret has indeed found rest here.

The manor house itself is said to be the scene of another haunting. A small boy in Victorian dress is sometimes seen scampering and playing around the main hall and the staircase. This unfortunate child died when he tumbled down the stairs while playing with another youngster of similar age. Like the much older Countess Margaret, he seems happy enough. Perhaps he spends eternity playing games.

GREAT MISSENDEN

The Black Monk of Missenden is one of the most famous ghosts in Buckinghamshire. Stories about him in Great Missenden are legion and it would almost seem that this phantom takes a positive delight in popping up around the village and giving locals – and visitors – a fright.

The centre of the hauntings is said to be the Abbey, which lies just off the High Street towards the southern end of the village. In medieval times this was a wealthy Augustinian monastery that owned vast estates in the area. As with all such religious houses, Great Missenden was founded on the principles of holiness, poverty and prayer. But the Black Monks of Missenden did not stick to their principles for long.

With their affairs prospering and increasing wealth pouring into the Abbey, the monks acquired a taste for luxury and loose living. The brothers became

The Abbey at Great Missenden, now a conference centre.

accustomed to slipping out of the Abbey by means of a secret tunnel that led to a tavern in the village. There they discarded their habits and dressed in fashionable clothing, before riding off to enjoy themselves in the fleshpots of London. The phantom Black Monk is said to be one of these spectacularly worldly sinners.

By the 1530s the growing scandal could not be suppressed any longer. Missenden found itself one of the first to be closed down by King Henry VIII in his Dissolution of the Monasteries.

The Black Monk is supposed to wander the grounds of the Abbey and the water meadows to the south. Walking with downturned head and slow footsteps, he plods across the grass at all hours of the day and night. He may head east towards the church of Saint Peter and Saint Paul. Built in the 15th century, this was the village church, but the monks sometimes went there to preach. Some claim the ghost is carrying a sword, which would make him sinful even by the standards of the monks of Missenden Abbey, but others say what he holds is a staff.

The people of Great Missenden know that the village itself also plays host to this wide-ranging phantom. In the 1970s a glazier at work on a property in the High Street saw a figure dressed in black enter the room on which he was working, although the house was locked and empty. The streets just around the George Inn are a favourite haunt for the ghost, though here he is most often glimpsed at night and only indistinctly. The George dates back to the 15th century, so perhaps this is the tavern where the monks would change their clothing.

Missenden Abbey is these days a conference centre and venue for weddings, birthday parties and the like and is not open to the general public. The current

The main street of Great Missenden where a ghostly figure in black startled a workman in the 1970s.

*The water meadows south of Great Missenden are said to be the
favourite haunt of the phantom Black Monk.*

manager is clear that no ghost has been seen in recent years. However, a public
footpath does run around the grounds and from here you can see the meadows
where the Black Monk was formerly at his most active.

CHENIES

I n the village of Chenies, to the north-east of Amersham, is Chenies
Manor House, an ancient building which for a few years in the 16th
century was near the hub of national life. King Henry VIII stayed here
with his new bride Anne Boleyn in 1533. These were happy days for Henry
and Anne, passed in loving passion, but soon Henry tired of Anne who

presented him with only a girl, the future Elizabeth I, not the boy he wanted as an heir. Anne was followed as a guest here by Henry's fifth wife, the lovely Catherine Howard who, like Anne, ended her life on the scaffold. Also a guest was Elizabeth when she was queen.

Chenies' days of glory came to an end in the Civil War when a troop of soldiers was billeted here. Thereafter the manor house slipped into a gentle rural obscurity that has allowed it to retain its period charm and style without being constantly updated and rebuilt, as is the fate of more fashionable houses. There have been periodic works, however, to update the building by introducing modern plumbing and electrics. It was during one such renovation in the 1970s that a small hidden chamber was found tucked into the thickness of an interior wall next to the Pink Bedroom. Inside, a tiny altar was discovered and, scratched into the walls, the date '9 September' in what seemed to be a 16th or 17th century hand.

The chamber was noted as a curiosity and left as it was. Which is when the hauntings began. The ghost has never been seen clearly enough to be identified. He appears only for an instant, then vanishes. The phantom is clearly a man, and is described as a heavily set person dressed in dark clothes. The only feature that those who see him can agree on is that he has a limp, seeming to drag one of his feet. Perhaps he is a Civil War soldier nursing a wound from one of the many skirmishes and battles that took place between the Royalist headquarters of Oxford and the fiercely Roundhead city of London.

Whoever the ghost may be, he does not like the door to his old room to be shut. The doors of the secret chamber and that of the Pink Bedroom are always found open no matter how carefully they are closed. The phantom's need for fresh air is as mysterious as his identity.

AMERSHAM

Amersham is one of these small English towns that has been developing and expanding in its own quiet fashion for centuries, each generation leaving its mark. It began as a market for the

The Chequers at Amersham is haunted by no less than nine ghosts.

surrounding villages, then gained fame for the production of quality wooden furniture and now is something of a dormitory town for commuters to London.

The broad High Street is lined by a curious mix of houses, shops and pubs that date from almost every decade back to the 16th century. Dominating the scene is the Market Hall, built by Sir William Drake in 1682. It is a unique structure with an open ground floor surrounded by lines of pillars supporting the upper storey in which are located the old offices of the market authorities and two stout cells for the imprisonment of any stallholder caught cheating with short measures or of market goers who imbibed a bit too heartily.

The pubs of Amersham reflect the town's long history. The Crown Inn has a wooden coat of arms that celebrates a visit by Elizabeth I. The King's Arms still retains its 16th century gables, while the Swan has a fine 17th century fireplace and chimney. But it is the Chequers that has the ghosts.

The Chequers public house stands on London Road West, not far outside the town centre. What makes this haunting so unusual is the nature of the ghosts to be found in this charming old inn and the frequency with which they are seen. There is not one ghost in the pub, but nine! Some are more active than others, of course, but they are all to be encountered with a rather alarming regularity.

The main part of the Chequers was built in about 1450, and a century later the gruesome events that led to the haunting took place. In those days religion was not a subject to be trifled with. Protestants regarded Catholics as traitors who sent money and secrets to that foreign despot, the Pope in Rome. The Catholics condemned the Protestants as agents of the Devil working to bring down the true church of Christ.

Passions ran high, and nowhere did they run higher than in Amersham. The townspeople were already inclining towards the Protestant faith when, in 1551, the fiery Scottish preacher John Knox paid a visit. Deeply religious and consumed by a burning faith in his brand of Christianity, Knox was a preacher of devastating power. He had a clear effect on Amersham, where the town turned firmly to the Protestant faith.

In 1551 this change of faith was notable but not especially dangerous. England had a Protestant monarch in the shape of Edward VI. In his quieter moods Edward let his people worship as they chose, but as ill health consumed him, the King became less tolerant of the Catholics he thought threatened his life and his rule. Amersham, being Protestant, was left alone.

It would not be left alone for long.

In 1553 Edward died and was replaced on the throne by his older and staunchly Catholic sister, Mary I. The new Catholic authorities took a very dim view of Protestant 'troublemakers' in Amersham who made a point of asking awkward questions such as what had happened to their Bible, printed in English, and why so much English money should be sent to finance the Pope and his court.

What these 'troublemakers' needed, the authorities believed, was a good burning at the stake. Queen Mary sent a troop of armed soldiers to Amersham supplied with a list of the influential Protestants in the town, the leader of whom was one William Tylsworth. He and six other men were convicted of heresy in a court packed by Catholics and, moreover, surrounded by Mary's soldiers who fingered their weapons ominously if any juror so much as looked sympathetically at the accused. The hapless Tylsworth and his friends were condemned to be burnt at the stake in nearby Rectory Woods.

The men were hauled off to the Chequers, at that date one of the stoutest public buildings in Amersham. There they were kept locked up overnight in an outbuilding of the pub under the watchful eye of a man named Osman. Next day the men were led to their deaths. In a macabre twist, Tylsworth's own daughter, Joan, was forced at swordpoint to light the fire that was to kill her father and take him to martyrdom.

It is hardly surprising that the moans and groans of the Amersham Martyrs have continued to disturb this building ever since. At one time the groans were so loud and persistent that it was difficult to

The haunted chamber at the Chequers is the only bedroom not rented out to paying guests. The ghost appears by the window.

sleep at the inn. The chamber where the martyrs were held lies to the back of the pub and can be identified by its old wooden door – the other outbuildings having more modern doors. The moans are today less disturbing than they used to be, which is just as well for the pub does a thriving bed and breakfast business.

There is, however, one small room where paying guests are not put, and with good reason. This room is occasionally visited by a hooded woman dressed all in white. She is said to be the unhappy spirit of Joan, returning to grieve for the father she was forced to kill.

The room in question is used by the staff as a quiet spot where they can relax. There is a small bed on which to lie and a chair by the window in which to read.

The bar at the Chequers. The ghostly gaoler appears most often near the fireplace.

The white lady, when she appears, is seen standing by the window. She gazes out towards the woods where her father died. Although she might be expected to be a troubled and disturbing spirit, those who have seen her declare quite the opposite. The room and the ghost both exude a calm and restful atmosphere. Perhaps Joan has found peace and rest in her firmly held faith.

Rather different is the ghost that lurks in the bar itself. This is the persistent ghost of Osman, the gaoler, who has been condemned to return time and again to the site where he sent innocent martyrs to their deaths. His cloaked figure is seen lurking near the fireplace in the front section of the bar. Not so long ago a new barman who knew nothing of the ghost asked the landlord about the man dressed in black he had seen apparently trying to climb the chimney. Was it a chimney sweep? No, it was Osman.

Ghosts apart, the Chequers is a fine example of an old country inn. The ancient fabric has not been too much altered over the years and the old timbers and beams add character to the bar.

WOODROW

ust to the west of Amersham, a tragic ghost is seen from time to time around the hamlet of Woodrow. This is Lady Helena Stanhope, better known today as the Green Lady of Woodrow. In the later 17th century, the Stanhopes were among the richest and most influential families in England. The head of the family had the title Earl of Chesterfield and was well respected at the court of Charles II.

Lady Helena was the daughter of the family and was well known as a beautiful and intelligent young lady. Combined with her wealth and family connections this made her a good marriage prospect and she attracted the attentions of England's richest bachelors. She chose, however, to give her heart to the dashing, handsome Sir Peter Bostock. Young and good-looking Sir Peter may have been, but as the younger son of a not terribly wealthy gentleman he did not measure up to the standard the Stanhopes expected for their daughter. Nevertheless he was a pleasant enough young man and so they did not turn him away completely. If only he could get some money together, he was informed, and so be able to keep Lady Helena in a manner befitting the dignity of the Stanhopes, the marriage could go ahead.

It was this ambition to gain wealth and so win the hand of his beloved that led Sir Peter into danger and in turn to the hauntings of Woodrow.

In 1685 Charles II died and was replaced on the throne by his brother James II. James was not a popular king. He was moody and difficult where Charles had been carefree and charming. He was prone to interfere too much in the government of his kingdom, overruling Parliament and nobles far more than his brother had done. And he was a Catholic who wanted to force his faith upon his Protestant subjects. By contrast, Charles's illegitimate son James, Duke of Monmouth, was very much like his father. He was popular, he was Protestant – and he was not James II.

Many people thought Monmouth would make a better king than his uncle, but since he was illegitimate he was not eligible. In June 1685 Monmouth sensationally produced papers that, he claimed, proved Charles had married his mother after all. That made him the true King of England. Monmouth landed in Lyme Regis with his documents, 82 men and a shipload of weapons. Thousands of men in the West Country rose to support the Protestant Duke and flocked to Monmouth's banner as he rode through Dorset, Wiltshire and Somerset, gathering an army.

Young Sir Peter Bostock saw in Monmouth his chance for happiness. If he joined Monmouth, Sir Peter reasoned, he could look for rich rewards when the Duke became king. Off he rode, having bid his beloved Lady Helena a fond farewell on the steps of Woodrow High House. Sadly for Sir Peter, Monmouth's force of raw recruits was caught by the professional royal army before the Duke had time to train his men. The resulting Battle of Sedgemoor was akin to a massacre, and the surviving rebels fled for their lives. Monmouth was captured, dragged to London and beheaded. His followers fared little better. Those caught in arms were summarily executed on the orders of the notorious 'Bloody Judge' Jeffreys, while men who had lent Monmouth money or supplies were sold into virtual slavery on the plantations of the West Indies.

Sir Peter spent several terrifying days on the run before he reached Woodrow and the arms of his Lady Helena. The Stanhopes were

The road from Amersham to Woodrow is haunted by a lady with a tragic history.

an influential family and, Lady Helena hoped, could save her beloved's life. First, however, the fugitive had to evade capture long enough for the vengeful wrath of King James to pass. Lady Helena hid Sir Peter in the little ornamental grotto in the grounds of the house, bringing him food when she could.

Alas for the lovers, they were betrayed. Word reached the royal army that the rebel Bostock was hidden somewhere near Woodrow. Scouts were sent to spy the land and soon glimpsed Lady Helena taking a package of food from High House to the grotto. As soon as she was gone, the soldiers pounced. Sir Peter was dragged off and, before the Stanhopes could intervene, was executed.

When Lady Helena found out that it had been she herself who had led the soldiers to Sir Peter's hiding place, she was overcome with remorse. One night soon afterwards, the servants heard a disturbance in the house. They hurried to the hall to find a cupboard broken open and Lady Helena lying dead, having drunk poison.

King James II ordered the summary execution of the fugitive of Woodrow.

To this day the High House, now home to the National Federation of Boys' Clubs, and the surrounding area are haunted by the Green Lady of Woodrow. This is a most eerie phantom. The ghost is described as being that of a tall and remarkably beautiful woman dressed all in green. What makes her particularly disturbing is the green glow that illuminates not just her but also everything around her. As she walks down the lane from High House to the

JAMES II.

lost grotto, the road surface, grass verges and roadside bushes are all bathed in a strange green light.

The ghost has also been seen in High House itself. The most dramatic, and best recorded, sighting came in 1946 when a team of workmen were living in the then run-down mansion while converting it for the use of the Federation. One workman woke up in the middle of the night, hearing somebody moving around downstairs. Fearing it might be some thief out to steal the valuable tools and materials lying around, the workman got up to investigate.

Silently creeping down the stairs, he was startled to see a woman dressed in green walking slowly along the corridor. At first he took the figure for a real woman, but she ignored his calls as she walked across the hall and, to his horror, passed straight through the window that had formerly been the front door of the house. Now thoroughly disturbed, the workman saw the ghost glide across the grounds to vanish on the edge of some woods.

The man raced back upstairs to the room where he and his workmates were sleeping. His sudden, agitated arrival woke up his colleagues who demanded to know the reason for the midnight fuss. The report was passed on to the owners of the new house who soon became aware of the story of the phantom Green Lady from villagers. It was decided there was little that could be done about the ghost and the work proceeded. The Green Lady has been glimpsed several times since, but she does nothing to disturb the good work of the Federation. She merely gives those who see her a bit of a start.

HUGHENDEN

At the top of Hughenden Valley, north of West Wycombe, lies Four Ashes Road. The area is perhaps best known for its scenic views, and as the site of the local cemetery and crematorium. But in the 1980s it acquired a far more sinister reputation for quite different reasons.

On 20th September 1986 a man from High Wycombe was driving his girlfriend home late one evening when they had a most unexpected encounter. As they drove along Four Ashes Road a huge figure loomed into view beside the road. It seemed to be a man dressed completely in green, and standing well over six feet tall. As the young couple approached, the figure turned to face them and began waving its arms. Thinking the strange man might be in trouble, the driver slowed down. At that point the green man stepped into the road, glared at the couple and then vanished into thin air.

It was a disturbing encounter. The young man reported what had happened to the local press. When the story was printed it prompted a number of other people to contact the newspaper to report that they had had similar experiences along the same stretch of road, but had kept quiet for fear of ridicule. In all cases, the tall green man was reported to be walking or standing beside the road, then to become agitated and wave his arms around before stepping into the road. Some thought the figure was being threatening, others that he was gesturing for help, but all agreed that he waved and leapt about with great vigour before abruptly vanishing.

It was not long before theories began to circulate to explain the strange sightings. The most obvious idea was that the tall man in green was the ghost of somebody buried at the cemetery. However, since nobody came forward to claim that a relative dressed in green had been buried recently, that idea faded.

Next was the idea that the figure was linked to a ley line that ran past the spot. Ley lines are formed when a number of mystic sites form a straight line on the map. These may include prehistoric stone circles, ghost sightings, legendary features and the like. In this case the ley

Not far from the haunt of the green man of Hughenden stands this appropriately named pub.

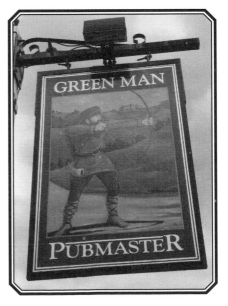

78

line's most enigmatic feature was the Witch's Stone at Speen, a few miles to the north. This stone was widely rumoured to be the site of meetings by local witches and, moreover, was said to cover a buried treasure. Ley lines are not accepted as being real by all; some believe that the sites are spread randomly across England and the straight lines are only a coincidence.

Finally, the discussion in the local press came to the conclusion that the strange phantom was the Green Man of old English folklore. This Green Man was the guardian spirit of the forests and of nature. He was said to have the power to regenerate himself if killed, as nature regenerates in spring, and to draw his strength from the beauty of the natural world around him.

There are dozens of stories about the Green Man from across Britain. He features in the classic medieval King Arthur story, Gawain and the Green Knight, and in local folk tales too numerous to mention. Why this ancient and powerful nature spirit should lurk along Four Ashes Road in the later 20th century is unclear. The countryside is scenic enough, but the plough has long since done away with any real wild woods from which he might draw strength.

The identity of the great green man of Hughenden must remain a mystery.

* * *

Very different is Hughenden's other ghost, for his identity is clearly known. This is Benjamin Disraeli, the great Conservative prime minister of the 19th century, who haunts his old home at Hughenden Manor.

Disraeli was born into a Jewish family, but was baptised a Christian and so was eligible to sit in the House of Commons. First, however, he had a successful career as a lawyer in the City of London and then gained fame as a popular novelist. With his fortune secure, Disraeli entered Parliament as the MP for Maidstone in 1837. He admired and respected the institutions that had made Britain great, but at the same time saw the need for reform. This combination of radicalism and conservatism was dubbed 'Young England' and marked Disraeli throughout his career. After an impressive showing both in cabinet and in opposition, he became Prime Minister for the first time in 1868.

Disraeli introduced many reforms designed to boost free trade and oppose protectionism. He also guided through the political Reform Act of 1867, which greatly extended the right to vote to poorer men, and he was careful not to allow the Empire to embark on any adventurous wars. In 1880 he retired from politics and returned to writing for the final year of his life.

Hughenden Manor provided a constant source of rest in Disraeli's busy life in politics and writing. It is therefore no surprise that he returns here in spectral form. The ghostly Disraeli is seen most often on or near

The Victorian Prime Minister Benjamin Disraeli still visits his old home at Hughenden.

the staircase, usually holding a sheaf of papers or files in his hand. More rarely he appears near his portrait in the main hall. Whenever he is seen, the ghost appears standing quite still and vanishes after only a few seconds. He is, it would seem, content just to stand and stare at his old home, now so carefully preserved by the National Trust.

WEST WYCOMBE

The most active ghost in West Wycombe, and possibly the most active in Buckinghamshire, is to be found at the George and Dragon. This is a most cheerful and fun-loving phantom, though her story is more tragic than happy.

In the 1730s the George and Dragon was one of several inns in West Wycombe catering for the coaching trade. What is now the A40 was then the Gloucester Road that ran from London, by way of Oxford, through Gloucester and on into South Wales. It was one of the busiest coaching routes in the kingdom, carrying rich merchants, dashing army officers and humble folk alike.

And one of the George and Dragon's prime attractions was young Sukie – an acknowledged beauty and a notorious flirt, although aged only 16. Her pretty face, attractive figure and sparkling wit kept the male travellers entertained and encouraged them to part with their money.

Although Sukie was adept at flirting with the men, she was no wanton. She knew the value of her honour and was determined to keep it until the right man came along. And for Sukie the right man was one of the rich, dashing travellers who would be able to whisk her away from her dull life as a serving wench and keep her in the manner to which she wished to become accustomed. Although the local farmhands and yeomen tried their hand at courting Sukie, she made it very clear she was not interested in them.

The George and Dragon at West Wycombe, haunted by a most attractive phantom.

She was, however, very interested in a rather mysterious traveller who stopped at the George and Dragon from time to time. He always travelled alone, mounted on a magnificent and clearly expensive stallion. His clothes were of the finest cut and most lavish fabric. And, unlike some others, he did not talk about a wife and family at home. Some gossiped that he was most likely a highwayman, but Sukie saw in him a very definite prospective husband – and a wealthy one at that.

After a few visits, it was clear the stranger was interested in Sukie. After yet more visits he proposed to the delighted girl. He promised that he had only to

The bay window from which Sukie would watch for her wealthy suitor.

tie up a few bits of loose business in London and he would send for her to join him. Sukie believed that she was as good as married and rich. Unfortunately she then became somewhat arrogant and patronising to her colleagues, and used her wit cruelly on three local men who had fancied themselves as would-be suitors.

The men were humiliated and angry, and plotted their revenge. They sent Sukie a message, pretending it came from the handsome stranger, proposing marriage and asking her to meet him at a chalk cave a short distance outside town. She was, the message said, to wear her finest dress as if for a wedding service.

When she received the note, the delighted Sukie hurriedly packed her bags, donned her most expensive gown and hurried off. But when she reached the cave, all she met were the taunts and jeers of the rejected suitors. Humiliated in her turn, Sukie burst into tears, turned and fled.

But as she ran, she tripped and knocked her head hard on a boulder. The men who had lured her to the cave hurriedly picked up the senseless body and carried it back to the George and Dragon. A doctor was called, but it was no use. Sukie died next morning. A few days later, she was buried in the churchyard to the general grief of West Wycombe.

Within a week, Sukie was back.

Unless you had known the poor girl was dead, there was nothing about Sukie to indicate she was not alive and full of fun. She tossed her long blonde hair as flirtatiously as ever, and bobbed through the inn with all her accustomed grace and charm. Pots and pans went missing, and tankards were moved around when nobody was looking. There was no doubt about it Sukie was back, and as the passing centuries have shown, she was back to stay.

To this day, Sukie with the long blonde hair is seen from time to time around the George and Dragon. Things go missing, only to turn up later somewhere else. Despite her tragic end, the young girl is still enjoying her time at her old place of employment.

* * *

Not far from the centre of town lies West Wycombe Park, a house and estate firmly linked to the name of one of the most notorious rakes and debauchees ever to live in England. Sir Francis Dashwood inherited the estate of West Wycombe from his father, along with an enormous fortune. It was, Dashwood decided, time to have some fun. He started by transforming his home into a spacious mansion built in the fashionable Palladian style. In 1741 he entered Parliament and quickly achieved a reputation for having a needle-sharp political instinct and first-rate intellect. He equally as quickly became known as a drunken libertine of heroic proportions.

Teaming up with Lord Orford, Lord Sandwich and John Wilkes, Dashwood established the Hell Fire Club, a society dedicated to orgies, drunkenness, gambling and political ambition. It proved to be a heady and successful mix. Orford was the son of Prime Minister Robert Walpole, and had extensive social contacts in society, while Wilkes owned a newspaper through which the group disseminated their views.

Sandwich proved to be the most successful of the group, and the only one to achieve anything of lasting good to the nation. He rose to the top in politics, serving in the cabinet for the first time in 1748 and holding high office until 1782. His great innovation, however, was to put a slice of cold roast beef between two slices of buttered bread and so invent the snack that still carries his name. Dashwood meanwhile became Chancellor of the Exchequer in 1762, apparently after impressing several MPs by being able to divide up a complex tavern bill despite being so drunk he could not stand.

It was the very next year that the Hell Fire Club broke up. A black mass was being enacted by the group after they had enjoyed a drunken dinner that had ended in the company of prostitutes. Orford was due to lead the prayers, and Dashwood had a surprise in store. He had dressed a baboon in the costume of the Devil and hidden it beneath a trap door. When Orford was reaching the climax of his prayers, the baboon was released. In the ensuing mayhem Orford temporarily – his critics said permanently – lost his mind.

With such a history it is unsurprising that West Wycombe is haunted. Dashwood himself is seen occasionally riding hell for leather up the steep hill towards West Wycombe church. Members

The hilltop church at West Wycombe, surmounted by its golden globe, where the Hell Fire Club held some of their bizarre events.

of his Hell Fire Club are known to have played cards in the ball on top of the church tower, and are rumoured to have indulged in less than sacred acts within the church itself.

The Music Room at the house is haunted by a lady. She is thought to be the grandmother of Sir Francis Dashwood, a lady every bit as gentle and loving as her grandson was the opposite.

But the most often seen ghost in West Wycombe House is that of a monk. Clearly dating from before the great rebuilding by Sir Francis, this figure stands quietly on the ground floor, smiling gently at visitors to the house. He does,

The mausoleum of Sir Francis Dashwood – politician, wit, debauchee and ghost.

perhaps, have something to smile about. While the worldly ambitions and spurious dark magic of Dashwood and his Hell Fire Club have passed away, the Christian Church remains.

* * *

The only other house of any great moment in the vicinity was Loakes House, closer to High Wycombe than to West Wycombe. In contrast to the scandalous goings on at West Wycombe Park, the lifestyle at Loakes House was the model of respectability. The house was not, however, without its share of tragedy. In the 1720s a young lady was killed just outside the gates in a riding accident. Her ghost returns here still. Riding a fine chestnut horse, the lady in a grey dress gallops up Loakes Road, then vanishes outside the gates where she met with her fatal accident. There is no sound of hoofbeats or any other noise at all. The ghost moves in absolute silence.

FINGEST

The ghost that lurks in the churchyard at Fingest, and wanders the road leading to the manor, is a harmless soul. Dressed as a forester or gamekeeper from centuries gone by, he is reported to walk quietly when he does not realise he is seen, but once he catches sight of somebody he bustles up to them as if to ask a favour, only to vanish abruptly.

The ghost might be almost anyone, but local legend has it that this is no humble gamekeeper. This is the ghost of Bishop Henry Berghersh of Lincoln who did much wrong hereabouts in his lifetime.

Back in 1321 the manor of Fingest belonged to the Bishopric of Lincoln, providing a comfortable stopping place when the bishops were travelling the country. Bishop Berghersh wished to enclose the open valley lands between Hanger Wood and possibly also Mill Hanging Wood and take it into his estates. This would have linked the divided lands and made a useful area for hunting deer when the good bishop was entertaining nobility or royalty.

The lane leading from the church at Fingest to the disputed land that gave rise to the haunting.

The problem was that the valley floor was common land on which the villagers of Fingest grazed their cattle and sheep. They did not much like having 300 acres taken away from them, leaving just 100 acres on which to graze their livestock. Dislike turned to great discontent when a series of poor harvests led to hunger. While neighbouring villages had livestock, milk and cheese, the folk of Fingest had nothing. There were fights and riots and the boundaries of the bishop's new lands were broken down.

In 1343 Bishop Berghersh finally decided that the villagers had a case, and decided to allow them once again to graze their livestock on the old common lands. But he then promptly died before his orders could be put into effect. In the confusion of electing a new bishop, the instructions concerning Fingest were forgotten and the enclosing bank and ditch left intact.

It seems that Bishop Berghersh died with a troubled conscience for only days later his ghost was met by his squire. The ghost, the squire reported, was clad in green and carried the tools of the forester. The phantom bishop announced that he had been condemned to act as the ghostly forester of Fingest until his orders were carried out and the villagers were again allowed to use their common land. The squire hurried off to the church authorities at Lincoln, who promptly ignored his story as being too far fetched to consider.

Back in Fingest, events moved on. The Black Death struck England, killing a third of the population and causing disruption across the land. While the disputed lands remained enclosed, the villagers quietly dug breaches in the bank to allow their livestock through. The clergy of Lincoln were too busy with their own affairs to pay much attention to what happened in distant Buckinghamshire. The good folk of Fingest regained access to their lands, but poor Bishop Berghersh was not freed from his penance.

The ghost of a man dressed in sturdy green clothes has been reported walking from the manor to the church, and in the churchyard itself. If this is Bishop Berghersh, he might be expected to spend more time patrolling the disputed lands. But perhaps his penance has been lifted enough so that he can visit the church to pray for forgiveness. It has, after all, been a long time and his sins were not really that bad.

MARLOW

Nestling beside the Thames, Marlow is one of the most scenic towns in Buckinghamshire. There are old houses, a weir over which the Thames tumbles in delightfully picturesque fashion and the surrounding countryside is very attractive. Unfortunately, the ghosts are not so charming.

The most persistent phantom is the bloody woman of Upton Court. This house is now an office complex, and its grounds have been converted into a park and sports area for the use of the citizens of Marlow. It is on Friday evenings that the ghost is seen most often, lurking beside the long straight path that runs past the children's playground towards the Thames.

This disturbing ghost is of a woman dressed in a long cream or white dress. She sobs and cries in a heart-rending fashion. This may be upsetting enough,

A game of rugby is played out in the grounds of Upton Court where a bloodstained ghost walks.

but it is her appearance that really has the power to shock. The front of her dress is bathed in blood, which

The strange coach and four that races towards Marlow on some unknown quest of great haste.

soaks the entire fabric and drips to the ground. It is a truly gruesome sight.

Who this ghost may be is unknown, but it is generally believed that she is connected in some way with Upton Court. She is said to appear most often close to the house, and on occasion in the house itself. The oldest part of the house dates back to the 15th century when it was the central manor of a large estate owned by Merton Abbey.

In comparison the otherwise alarming phantom of Frieth Road is almost tame. This ghostly coach and four lumbers down the hill towards Marlow, the horses sweating with the exertion of pulling their load at the high speeds demanded of them. Lurching from side to side and appearing in imminent danger of a catastrophic crash, the coach rushes on its course oblivious to any pedestrians or vehicles that may be in its path. Who this coach might belong to, and why it is in such a rush, are questions as obscure as the identity of the bloodstained woman of Upton Court.

CHALFONT ST GILES

A passing traveller could be forgiven for thinking that Chalfont St Giles was a sleepy little English village. There is an ancient stone church, a green, a collection of charming old cottages and a number of modern houses. The village presents a quaint, rustic face to the world.

But the folk of Chalfont St Giles are rather more adventurous than the façade might suggest. The poet John Milton wrote most of his greatest works while living in a small cottage here. *Paradise Lost* was completed after he had left London in disgust at the reinstatement of the monarchy after the rule of Oliver Cromwell and his victorious generals. Milton had planned the epic poem as a tribute to the triumph of the Godly, an allegory of the victory of the Puritans in the aftermath of the Civil War, but the restoration of the King and

The White Hart at Chalfont St Giles, where a former landlord plays a ghostly violin.

a less strict version of Protestantism plunged him into despair. Life in Chalfont St Giles obviously agreed with the poet as he eventually cheered up enough to write *Paradise Regained*. This second work is still sombre and grave but looks forward to the triumph of faith and reason over passion and haste.

This little village also attracted Captain James Cook and, much later, Bertram Mills. The former stayed at a house named The Vache in between voyages of exploration to the South Seas. Although not of the poetic turn of mind of Milton, Cook immortalised the house by giving its name to a Pacific island. Not much remembered these days, Bertram Mills developed the circus in its modern form – from which he made so much money that he became a generous philanthropist in Buckinghamshire. He is buried in St Giles' churchyard.

In the years before the Great War of 1914 to 1918, these connections to the famous brought as many people to Chalfont St Giles as did the village's rural charms. The place of choice for visitors to stay was the old White Hart, in the heart of the village. No doubt the clean rooms and good food were attractions, but the star of the place was the landlord Donald Ross, who was famous far and wide as a character, attracting guests to his inn with his anecdotes, jokes and general bonhomie. Among his more famous skills was his playing of the violin. Ross was no mere rustic fiddler, scraping out folk tunes on his instrument. He was an accomplished musician who prided himself on being able to perform any tune named by a guest, or at least to follow their humming with skill.

In the 1920s Mr Ross passed away. His music did not. Within a few weeks of his death, the violin was heard again, its faint notes drifting through the inn. At first it was thought that a radio might be playing, or that some prankster was at work. But gradually such explanations were discarded and yet the music played on. The violin is not heard so often these days, but its plaintive notes will sometimes whisper around when the bar is quiet and more modern electronic music does not dominate.

Perhaps the famous Donald Ross still cares for the entertainment of guests at his old inn.

CHALFONT ST PETER

The former coaching inn at Chalfont St Peter, the Greyhound, has an interesting and colourful history. Before railways were invented, the only way to get around the country was to travel by horse-drawn coach. The roads were, on the whole, fairly dreadful so speeds were slow. In summer the dust kicked up by the horses' hooves and the coach wheels was choking. In winter the unheated coach was often bitterly cold. Those passengers who chose the cheap seats on the roof would be given large, heavy cloaks as protection, and sometimes found themselves frozen to the coach.

A stop at a comfortable hostelry, such as the Greyhound Inn, would be more than welcome. While the horses were being changed, boys and staff would swarm to the passengers. Hammers and chisels would be produced to free those frozen in place, while hot drinks and plates of appetising food were on offer – for a suitable price, of course.

It is one such scene that is played out in spectral form in the High Street of Chalfont St Peter, close to the Greyhound. A phantom stagecoach suddenly appears on the Amersham road, the coachman swathed in a thick

The haunted stretch of road beside the Greyhound at Chalfont St Peter.

cloak and the shapes of outside passengers perched on top. The coach would appear to be of the early 18th century, and it is clearly travelling in deep winter if the thick clothes of the coachman are anything to go by.

The coach comes around the corner to enter the High Street, ignoring the modern bypass. It pulls to a halt outside the Greyhound. The coachman puts down the reins and his whip, glances towards the inn – and then the whole apparition vanishes. Perhaps, with his ghostly journey done, the coachman has completed his task.

There are no stories of any tragedies or triumphs that might explain this particular haunting. It is simply as if the journey is over – at least until the phantom coach begins its travels again somewhere on the Amersham road.

GERRARDS CROSS

The woooded lanes east of Gerrards Cross are peaceful enough – usually. But on dark, moonless nights visiting them can be quite startling.

It is at times such as this that the mysterious glowing horseman is at large, riding in total silence and emitting a spookily green aura that illuminates not just himself, but also the trees nearby. One witness who saw the ghost in the 1980s said that he wore a hat and had a cloak billowing out behind him. Other descriptions are more vague, which is not surprising given the

The mysterious horseman of Gerrards Cross dresses in clothes of the 18th century, according to one witness.

circumstances. All that can be said with any real certainty is that the horseman comes from nowhere, gallops past at high speed and then is gone.

He seems to prefer the warm nights of summer to the chill of winter, but otherwise his activities are fairly non-specific. He may appear on almost any road in the area and has been reported galloping in a variety of directions.

FULMER

The phantom carriage of Fulmer is one of those enigmatic apparitions that simply seem to appear without any cause or reason. Nobody knows of any story why this ghostly vehicle should plague the village, nor is there any record of a crash or other misfortune that might explain it. The ghost just appears from time to time and that is all there is to it.

The ghostly carriage begins its journey south of the village on Framewood Road, heading north. It passes through Fulmer, trotting past the Black Horse Inn, then leaves along Fulmer Road towards Gerrards Cross. The purpose of the journey is as mysterious as the ghost itself.

A car negotiates the ford outside Fulmer, near which a phantom carriage begins its journey north.

•Index•